Y0-BCW-948

A PRIMER OF *Playwriting*

Writing for the theatre is a peculiar business. . . . It involves a craft that you have to learn and a talent that you must possess. Neither is common and both are essential.

GOETHE

A PRIMER OF

Playwriting

KENNETH MACGOWAN

RANDOM HOUSE • NEW YORK

First Printing

For permission to quote passages from their respective publications, grateful acknowledgment is made to the following authors and publishers:

Prentice-Hall, Inc.: Marian Gallaway, *Constructing a Play* (copyright, 1950, by Prentice-Hall, Inc.); Grosset & Dunlap: Arthur Edwin Krows, *Playwriting for Profit* (copyright, 1928, by Longmans, Green & Co.); Charles Scribner's Sons: Henrik Ibsen, *From Ibsen's Workshop* (copyright, 1911, by Charles Scribner's Sons); Vanguard Press and Paramount Pictures Corporation; Ferenc Molnar, *The Play's the Thing*, in *The Plays of Ferenc Molnar* (copyright, 1929, by Vanguard Press).

Published in New York by Random House, Inc., and simultaneously in Toronto, Canada, by Random House of Canada, Limited.

Manufactured in the United States of America by Kingsport Press, Inc., Kingsport, Tennessee

A. B.

To

EUGENE O'NEILL

and

ROBERT EDMOND JONES

and the theatre we worked for

CONTENTS

A PRIMER OF *Playwriting*

1

The Human Limitations

> God forbid that I should set up for a teacher! I purpose merely to confide to my readers what little I have learned . . . reminding them meanwhile that even in the least important books one sometimes finds small matters deserving attention.
>
> GOLDONI

Playwrights Born, Not Made

ALL THE NONSENSE ABOUT RULES FOR PLAYWRITING began with Aristotle. Horace did his bit, and then the archaeological maniacs of the Renaissance—who thought they were reproducing classic art and culture—distorted the wise observations of Aristotle on the nature of Greek tragedy, added ideas of their own to a large mass of misinterpretation, and tried, with some success, to put a strait jacket on the drama. Fortunately, Shakespeare and Lope de Vega and Molière paid no attention to the "classic" rules, as their happy audiences spurred them on to a drama answerable only to the people who went to the theatre. Then, as the European theatre changed through the centuries—

and the drama with it—new writers produced new theories and wrote down new rules and recipes for the drama of their own times, from Corneille and Dryden to Ibsen and Anderson. Scores of books and hundreds of articles now attest to the desire of some writers to teach, and of other writers to learn, an art that cannot, in the broadest sense, be taught or learned unless the student has a certain natural gift.

"Though there are a good many volumes on the art of playwriting," says Robert Finch in *How to Write a Play*, "it does not seem that the writing of plays has been much simplified . . . for like other fine arts playwriting cannot be taught. . . . The ability to write a successful play depends greatly upon the possession of a particular talent which is not capable of being imparted."

The cold fact of the matter is that playwrights are born, not made. Yet—and that is why books like this are written—a certain number of writers possess an innate and instinctive dramatic talent, and this talent can be quickened and expanded and guided toward a more rapid and effective expression in written drama.

Most human beings—perhaps all but those that would be safer and happier in an institution other than the theatre—have an instinct for imitation. They are indeed, as Aristotle put it, "the most imitative of living creatures." This instinct is the basis of education; and —along with a few feats of initiative such as the discovery of fire and the invention of the printing press

—it has led man up from *Pithecanthropus* to the wielder of the atomic bomb, creating the theatre on the way. An extension of this bent for mimicry—the peculiar and intense thing we call instinct for the theatre—is something the playwright must have; but he must, of course, have much, much more. It is not enough that he should be an inventor of good plots or a recorder and interpreter of human character. It is not enough that he should also be a master of dialogue. Besides all this, he must have a talent for the peculiar organization of plot, characters, and dialogue that creates the suspenseful and mounting excitement without which no audience is satisfied.

Dramaturgy in the Universities

How to use and heighten such a talent—which is the art of playwriting—has always been taught in the living theatre, but it has been taught by indirection. The observation of success and failure has served as a rule-of-thumb to the playwright's inspiration. Now for nearly fifty years playwriting has also been taught in a number of universities in the United States.

Professor George Pierce Baker introduced the first university course in playwriting at Radcliffe College—Harvard's discreet approach to co-education—in the spring of 1904, and a year and a half later he was permitted to teach the same course, English 47, at the older, more famous, and more conservative institution.

Ignoring the fact that Shakespeare and O'Casey got along quite well on something less than a decent grammar-school education, and that Ibsen and Shaw never had an academic degree between them, more than sixty universities in the United States have followed the lead of Harvard and have even outdistanced that cautious institution, which banished playwriting from the curriculum when Baker left for Yale in 1925. The output of university playwrights doesn't include a Shakespeare or a Molière, but it numbers more men of distinction than drank at the Mermaid Tavern or sat in the Hôtel de Bourgogne. No one can say what the future may make of Eugene O'Neill, Sidney Howard, Robert Sherwood, Philip Barry, Paul Green, S. N. Behrman, Tennessee Williams, and Arthur Miller, but there can be no question that their work under Baker, Fred Koch, Kenneth T. Rowe, or Marian Gallaway hastened their maturity and broadened their technical powers. Maxwell Anderson, who had had no Professor Baker at Stanford University, gave evidence in 1938 of what he feels a conscious study of dramatic form may do for a playwright:

> It was not until after I had fumbled my way through a good many successes and an appalling number of failures that I began to doubt the sufficiency of dramatic instinct and to wonder whether or not there were general laws governing dramatic structure which so poor a head for theory as my own might grasp and use . . . I began to search again among the theorists of the past for a word of

wisdom that might take some of the gamble out of playwriting. What I needed most of all, I felt, was a working definition of what a play is, or perhaps a formula which would include all the elements necessary to a play structure.

Tacitly recognizing his own innate and essential talent for playwriting, Anderson was saying in another way what Baker had said in his *Dramatic Technique* in 1919: " 'The dramatist is born, not made.' This common saying grants the dramatist at least one experience of other artists, namely, birth, but seeks to deny the instruction in art granted the architect, the painter, the sculptor, the musician."

Another teacher of playwriting, William Thompson Price, who opened a non-academic school for dramatists in New York in 1901, put it more simply: "What can be learned can be taught."

But a question remains, and it is a question inherent in the basic fact that a dramatist is indeed born, not made: just what *can* be learned and therefore what can be taught?

The Limits of Learning

Nobody can teach you how to write good dialogue. A teacher can only help you by pointing out occasional lapses, awkward repetitions of words, speeches that are not in character. He cannot teach you how to invent plots. He can only indicate flaws such as dullness, inconsistency, and anticlimax, and possibly suggest changes and developments that seem inherent in the material. A teacher cannot show you how to create characters. He can only call your attention to the stereotypes in your script, and suggest the need for richer and more significant detail. He cannot give you that inherent sense of the dramatic that stamps the natural-born playwright, but he can show you how you may have bungled in organizing the material you have brought together. Above all, he cannot teach you how to have something to say, but he can help you by sneering at your puerilities and platitudes, and trying to open your mind to the richness of human experience that lies all about you.

There are, however, certain technical aspects of playwriting—as there are of other arts—that can be taught directly and concisely. These are: (a) skill in exposition, (b) the knack of introducing facts and attitudes well ahead of scenes for which they are a kind of preparation, (c) the elimination of everything that destroys general emotional unity, (d) the development of successive crises, (e) the placing of the major climax well into the last portion of the play, (f) the development of conflicts of wills and circumstances, and (g) the use of complications to provide mounting suspense. Of these, the last four—crises, climax, conflict, and complications—cannot be taught a student who lacks dramatic instinct. In these lies the basic distinction between narrative and dramatic writing.

The teacher of playwriting may instill theories through lectures or through a book like this, and these theories may be of considerable help in the subsequent writing of a play. But really effective teaching—or at least the great bulk of it—can be done only through concrete criticism of a concrete play written by the student. And it can be done most effectively after that play has been produced in a workshop course or, at the worst, read aloud.

Precepts on playwriting may be too short and simple, and leave too much of a practical nature unsaid; I am thinking of a remark by the elder Dumas, "It's very simple: the first act clear, the last act short, and all the acts interesting." Few books on this subject are so dim-witted and so useless as Georges Polti's naïve listing of what he considered all plots, *The Thirty-Six Dramatic Situations.* Most books are not so effective as they might be because they try to teach too much and to teach things that cannot be taught, and they get deeply, obscurely, bewilderingly involved in philosophic and aesthetic theory. They are so elaborate and complex that they are of no use at all to the beginner and usually puzzling to the practiced playwright. J. M. Barrie, seeking to discover whether, as he characteristically put it, a fellow-dramatist "wrote his plays properly," confessed that he "cautiously bought a book about how to write plays . . . but the book was so learned, and the author knew so much, and the subject when studied grew so difficult, that I hurriedly abandoned my enquiry."

Oddly enough, the successful dramatist seldom writes about his art more significantly or intelligibly than the playgoing critic. Arthur Wing Pinero, John Galsworthy, J. M. Barrie, St. John Ervine, Langdon Mitchell, Jesse Lynch Williams, Samson Raphaelson, Philip Barry, and John Howard Lawson are, on the whole, neither better nor worse than George Pierce Baker, Arthur Edwin Krows, Lajos Egri, Kenneth Thorpe Rowe, Marian Gallaway, Samuel Selden, Alan Reynolds Thompson, and Robert Finch. William Archer, after translating much of Ibsen abominably and before writing *The Green Goddess*, had much to say that was pertinent and a little that was overelaborate and confusing. The ability to lay an egg seems to have little bearing on the making or savoring of an omelet.

The virtue of this book, if it has any, is that it strives to be no more than its title professes; it is indeed a primer. I cannot say that it should be the "first" book for the beginning playwright, but it is designed for him alone, and it is short. A great deal of its material is culled from other writers, though I have tried to add something from my experience as critic and producer. Its chief value resides in selection, condensation, and organization.

Seeing, Reading, and Working

Aside from reading a book like this and writing plays, there is much for a beginning playwright to do. He should go to the theatre as often as he can. I mean, of course, the playhouse with "round actors"—as a child at the Barter Theatre in Virginia once described flesh-and-blood players—not the motion-picture palace; for films are generally too loose, too narrative, in form. If the student lives in a town where touring companies seldom play, he will probably find a community theatre or a university theatre within reach. He can always read printed plays and he should read them assiduously. Whether he sees a play or reads it, he should be on the lookout for its virtues and its failings. After he has seen a play, he should read the script if he can get hold of it; for, while a performance reinforces dramatic virtues, it also hides failings. When you see *Oedipus Rex* you may never notice—and wonder—how Creon, Laius's old servant, and Oedipus's Corinthian benefactor all happen to turn up in Athens at the same time. At a performance of *Romeo and Juliet* you may not challenge the convenient "secret drug" that enables Juliet to give the appearance of death, or the still more convenient plague that prevented Friar John from reaching Romeo with the news that Juliet is taking the drug to avoid marriage with Paris (a device that could have been legitimatized if a Capulet had killed or delayed a Montague errand boy). When I first saw *Hamlet* I was not at all conscious of the fact that the people on the stage were not in agreement as to whether Ophelia had killed herself or been accidentally drowned.

Play reading makes analysis easier but, unless a play can be read after seeing a performance, it puts stumbling blocks in the path of complete enjoyment. As almost every writer on the theatre has said at some time or other, the script is only a portion of the play. The usual comparison is to say that the typed or printed play is to the performed play as a blueprint is to a finished building or a musical score to a symphony played by an orchestra. The ability and imagination of the director, the cast, and the scenic designer amplify or reshape the printed dialogue and stage directions, bringing out emotional values that lie hidden in the script. Even the audience plays an important part, for it may spur actors to finer and finer effects, or it may lead their efforts astray. The reaction of a full house that understands, appreciates, and enjoys a play will, obviously, excite actors to greater efforts. Sometimes, of course, during a long run the actors may consciously or unconsciously exaggerate certain effects in response to applause, and they may end by "hamming up" a performance at many points. A small audience will depress a company of actors, and the performance will lose drive and sparkle. When an audience does not understand a play, or a play does not make itself clear and sympathetic to an audience, there will be apathy among the spectators, or, worse still, laughter in the wrong place, and the performance will suffer. But whether an audience helps or hinders a play and its performance, an audience is vitally essential. As Jesse Lynch Williams once said: "A play really cannot be played without an audience to play it on. It would be like playing a piano without any strings." Three hundred and fifty years earlier, the Italian student of Aristotle, Lodovico Castelvetro, made much the same point: "Tragedy cannot effect its proper function with a reading, without staging and acting."

A man who has worked in the theatre will read a play with more understanding than one who has not. He will also write a better play, if he has it in him to write a play at all. A beginning playwright should join a producing group even if he only shifts scenery. At a university he should take as many theatre courses as he can—workshop courses and courses in direction, in particular—and he should participate in public performances, whether he acts or merely works on the stage crew. In the foreword to Marian Gallaway's *Constructing a Play*, Tennessee Williams, a former student of hers at the University of Iowa, writes:

I am not sure how much I actually learned in the classrooms and how much came to me by that process called osmosis, a gradual soaking-in that occurs involuntarily through the mere fact of exposure. It was perhaps more in the physical aspects of the theatre, the courses in stagecraft and the shopwork backstage, that I picked up the most valuable training. But I do know that I left Iowa City and my year's association with the author of this book with a great deal more theatre knowledge than I had brought there.

Williams might have added that he had learned the vitally important lesson that playwriting does not end in the author's study, but goes on through the whole co-operative business of actual production.

The living theatre is the playwright's laboratory. It is essential that the beginning playwright should actively work in it as well as take every opportunity to see its plays. Yet, while he immerses himself in the theatre, he must not lose contact with the world of life and the world of letters. A poor dramatist, as St. John Ervine, author of *John Ferguson,* has aptly put it, is "a man who goes into the theatre and never comes out of it. A good dramatist is a man who constantly checks the creatures of his imagination with the creatures he discovers about him." This applies to the apprentice playwright even more than to the practiced dramatist. In addition, the student must read widely and deeply. He must not only read novels, as well as plays; he must acquaint himself with enough of history, philosophy, and the social sciences to have more understanding than most men have of the society in which he and his characters live. Reading cannot destroy originality or imagination. Someone once said that the most original man in the world is the man with the best memory. Stock your memory with knowledge. You may be sure that Shakespeare, Molière, Ibsen, and Shaw read more avidly than most university students.

The Most Difficult of Techniques

No writing is easy. Only dogged determination drives most authors through the first hour and the first paragraphs of each day. Ervine calls playwriting "the hardest and most discouraging form of writing." A long play is a long job. On the average it contains as many words—about 30,000—as a long short story, or novelette; yet it has to contain, says Ervine, "as much substance as a full-length novel." Most writers agree that the novel is a far easier form for the beginner.

The play demands a clarity unmatched in any other kind of writing. "In most novels," wrote Baker, "the reader is, so to speak, personally conducted, the author is our guide. In the drama, so far as the dramatist is concerned, we must travel alone." A play is uniquely objective because the author must convey everything through the dialogue of living men and women, and has no opportunity for personal comment and description outside of printed stage directions. Acted on the stage, the play has complete objectivity, and, because of that, every line, every speech, every scene, must be crystal clear if it is ever to be understood. As you read a novel you can stop to think about a passage; if it proves too difficult, you can reread it. But in the theatre words race by like the moving letters of the news bulletin on the Times Building in New York. If you don't quite understand a speech or a scene, you have no time to think about it, for the next scene is already demanding your complete attention.

This need for clarity does more than ban the over-subtle as well as the confused. It demands judicious repetition. The Spanish playwright Benavente once said: "Everything that is of importance to the understanding of the play must be repeated at least three times during the course of the action. The first time half the audience will understand it. The second time the other half will understand it. Only at the third repetition may we be sure that everybody understands it, except, of course, deaf persons and certain critics." When other playwrights echo this theory of triple repetition they are stressing by exaggeration one of the most difficult aspects of a most difficult art.

Mob-art and Master-art

Because a play does not really exist without a production and an audience, the playwright is bound to test his success as an artist by the ability of his play to communicate. "The painter and the lyric poet," said John Galsworthy, "may deny any intent to communicate through their works; but the playwright who does so denies the very medium in which he professes to work." "The drama," wrote Archer in *Play-making*, "has no meaning except in relation to an audience." Another Englishman, the critic A. B. Walkley, called drama "a function of the crowd." "There is no dramatic art without success," writes Louis Jouvet, the French actor and director. "No dramatic work is valid unless it finds a public to listen to it and make it live. . . . The necessary yet blind collaboration of an audience, which is, at the same time, the object and the reason for dramatic work, subjects the theatre to the necessity to please." In the seventeenth century another Frenchman, Pierre Corneille, wrote: "The sole end of the drama is to please the audience." Dr. Samuel Johnson put it in rhyme:

The drama's laws the drama's patrons give
And we that live to please must please to live.

To the young idealist all this may smack of crass commercialism. But the nature of the theatre is such that the effective and therefore the successful presentation of a play creates potent values unique to this form of human activity. Here, though you strive for wide acceptance of what you write, there can be no thought of prostitution. The hardest task of all, the task that very few are equipped for, is to "write down" to an audience. Neither producer nor playwright can guess infallibly what the public wants. What it wanted yesterday is not what it will want tomorrow. The playwright must create and the manager produce what satisfies him. He must merely see that the material is not so special or so esoteric that only a few thousand will react to it. The theatre is no ivory tower.

The German philosopher and critic Georg Wilhelm Friedrich Hegel saw the necessity of writing for a wide public, but he also saw that this meant writing of great, eternal things, common to the playwright's time and nation. Today he would, I am sure, change "nation" to "world." August Wilhelm Schlegel said: "The dramatic poet [*Dichter,* or creative writer], more than any other, is obliged to court external favor and loud applause. But, of course, it is only in appearance that he thus lowers himself to his hearers; in reality, he is raising them to himself." Another German, Gotthold Ephraim Lessing, saw and admitted the demands of the audience and also saw and gloried in the power of the dramatist over his audience: "To what end the hard work of dramatic form? Why build a theatre, disguise men and women, torture their memories, invite the whole town to assemble at one place, if I intend to produce nothing more than some of those emotions that would be produced as well by any good story that anyone could read by his chimney-corner at home? The dramatic form is the only one by which pity and fear can be excited; at least in no other form can these passions be excited to such a degree." If Lessing had not been so absorbed in interpreting

Aristotle, he might well have included exaltation and laughter along with pity and fear.

If the play form seems arduous and intractable—as indeed it is—remember Goethe's words: "It is through the limitations of an art that the master shows his genius." Alan R. Thompson has put it in a different way in *The Anatomy of Drama:* "The more resistant the medium, other things being equal, the greater the impressiveness of a successful mastery of it."

Today—the Playwright's Theatre

For the dramatist, the American stage of today is a place of striking advantages and disadvantages.

"Today," says Kenneth T. Rowe in *Write That Play,* "we are in the playwright's theatre. . . . The play used to be the actor's vehicle, now the actor is the play's interpreter. It is a symbol of two generations that James O'Neill, the father, was nationally known as an actor, and Eugene O'Neill is a national figure as a dramatist." The star was still regnant in 1906 when Langdon Mitchell, son of the distinguished novelist and physician S. Weir Mitchell, wrote his witty comedy, *The New York Idea,* for Mrs. Minnie Maddern Fiske; but, within twenty years, the dramatist had so dominated the American stage—as he had dominated the European long before—that Mitchell could say: "The playwright is now for the first time in three centuries a respectable person." Further, new American plays and our plays of the past three decades are now widely produced in the Old World theatre.

On the other hand, the Broadway theatre—toward which practically all playwrights consciously or unconsciously aim—has shrunk drastically in the past twenty years, as motion pictures, radio, and television have taken over playhouse after playhouse, and no new ones have been built. When I was a drama critic in the 1920's there were almost four times as many theatres in New York as there are now. The following figures from an article, "America's Endowed Theatre," by Hubert Heffner, tells the same story over a shorter area of time:

	THEATRES	PRODUCTIONS	NEW PLAYS
1927–28	80	302	205
1937–38	39	110	69
1947–48	31	89	43

In early April of 1951 only 24 legitimate theatres were open.

"Of the six writers' mediums," says Paul R. Reynolds in his book *The Writing Trade,* "the one that is hardest to break into, the one which requires the greatest amount of ability and skill for success on the part of the writer, is the Broadway theatre. . . . All writers' mediums have a gambling element, but the play business is the most speculative of all concerned." As the number of Broadway productions has shrunk, however, the returns to the playwrights in terms of longer runs and larger incomes have greatly increased. A year's engagement—much more common now than in the past—means $100,000 in royalties, with the chance of an additional return, as great or greater, from the movie rights.

On the good side, it is clear that the quality of the plays produced has, on the average, much increased. The obvious melodrama and the cheap farce have almost disappeared under Hollywood's competition. The New York stage has always had room for the experimental, the unconventional. *The Yellow Jacket* and *Sumurun* in 1912, Molnar's *The Phantom Rival* in 1914 and his *Liliom* in 1921; the Hopkins-Barrymore-Jones productions of Tolstoi's *Redemption, Richard III*, and *Hamlet; The Emperor Jones, The Hairy Ape, The Great God Brown*, and *Desire Under the Elms*—all four coming uptown from Greenwich Village—*Strange Interlude* and *Mourning Becomes Electra*, many another Theatre Guild production, and *The Green Pastures* only foreshadowed the high standards in playwriting and production and the freedom to experiment with new dramatic forms that have brought to Broadway, since 1938, distinguished successes like *Our Town, The Little Foxes, The Skin of Our Teeth, The Glass Menagerie, All My Sons, A Streetcar Named Desire, The Death of a Salesman, The Member of the Wedding, The Lady's Not for Burning*, and *The Rose Tattoo.*

For the theatre of today and tomorrow, the golden

rule—as Shaw said forty years ago on another topic—is that there is no golden rule.

This does not mean that the apprentice playwright should shoot at the experimental moon. He must learn to walk the road of conventional dramaturgy before he can safely run the byways of theatrical experimentation. Picasso was a master of draftsmanship before he began to experiment with cubism. Apprenticeship is the time to learn how to use tested tools, not to search out new techniques; that will come with time and experience. Try first to master the solid three-act play. Learn all practical skills. Some will apply to one play, some to another. Many of them—and you cannot tell which—will prove of the greatest assistance when you strike out to write a play as fresh in treatment as *The Death of a Salesman.* Miss Gallaway summarizes this well: "The apprentice playwright should practice the use of these tools as the young pianist does his scales. He should master them as *tools,* as devices to use in solving problems, not as rules which he must follow. These tools do not substitute for the qualities of the artist; but to master them may save the artist time, energy, and the heartbreaking frustration of working by the trial-and-error method."

"We must be on our guard," as Alan Thompson says, "against a tendency to condemn all artifices of the theatre along with the cruder ones. In a broad sense all plays are nothing but artifices." This is a word of needed caution for the young writer to whom, as

Archer put it, "even the most innocent tricks of emphasis are snares of the evil one."

All this talk of technique does not mean that the beginner can or should ignore content. He must guard, of course, against thinking that sound argument makes drama, or that a play can live by characters alone or by consummate wit. But all the craftsmanship in the world means nothing without sound substance, truth to human character, emotion or laughter which tells us something about life that we want to know and need to know. Master the skills, but don't rate them above content. Stylistically Kipling wrote better than Dickens, and he plotted more skillfully. But the characters and the humanity and the indignation of Dickens will long be remembered, while Kipling is now almost forgotten.

2

Definitions, or the Art of Confusion

It is certain that there are laws of the drama, since it is an art; but it is not certain what these laws are.

CORNEILLE

. . . the mastery of drama is further complicated by the fact that, being an art, it simply is not governed by a set of laws.

FINCH

Twenty-three Centuries of Confusion

CONFLICTS LIKE THIS BETWEEN CORNEILLE AND FINCH are typical of the whole business of analyzing the craft of the playwright and trying to find rules to govern it. The confusions that have developed in the twenty-three hundred years since Aristotle wrote his *Poetics* are both basic and superficial. They arise from the difficulty of defining what drama really is and how a play is manufactured, and these confusions are worse confounded by the inordinate passion of certain critics for the kind of verbal pottage that is made up of six-bit words of Greek and Latin origin, new meanings for old terms, and obscure phraseology. When Polonius asked Hamlet, "What do you read, my lord?" and he replied, "Words, words, words," I shrewdly suspect that the melancholy Dane, having decided to feign madness, was reading a treatise on playwriting. In this chapter I shall attempt to straighten out or to dissipate some of the confusions and complications and needless distractions that have been added to more or less sensible thinking on a difficult subject.

Take the words "crisis" and "climax." To the average human, a crisis seems smaller than a climax. That idea appeals also to many critics, and these analysts of playwriting suggest that a number of crises lead to the main climax of a drama. Others have discovered, however, that climax comes from a Greek word κλῖμαξ, meaning "ladder," and so they decide that the climax is not the pinnacle of the plot—or, as the *Century Dictionary* defines it, "the highest point of intensity"—but that, instead, it is the rise in intensity that leads us to the pinnacle. And the pinnacle—which most poor innocents call the climax—becomes the crisis. Not to be outdone, somebody else says that "climax" is what we usually call "resolution"—the resolution of the plot, not the resolution in the soul of some character or other. The next difficulty is that there can be many major and minor crises and many major and minor climaxes, and one writer has actually counted 100 crises and 28 climaxes in *Elizabeth the Queen*—which doesn't simplify matters much for the beginning playwright.

Many of us have been using the word "complication" to mean a factor that crops up to jolt the plot along into new suspense when the old excitement is in danger of dying. But somebody else thinks that a complication is a struggle set up by interfering with the will of the hero, not the factor that starts a new struggle. Then words and phrases like "the attack" appear, and "precipitation of the conflict," and "inciting moment," and "consciousness of significance," and "the projection of the major dramatic question" ("question," by the way, is just a new way of saying "suspense").

Every little while a writer turns up with new words like "pointers." A pointer is a "tantalizing glimpse of what may happen," and it may take the form of a direct statement—or the lack of a statement—a threat, a sense of impending character clash, or a piece of business. Then there is a "plant," which differs from a "pointer" because it makes the audience look back to it as a justification, instead of ahead in anticipation. I suppose there is no great harm in splitting the older word "preparation" in half in this fashion, but it is a symptom of the mania for the manufacture and multiplication of terms that ends in more and more confusion for the young.

For example, after learning without too much difficulty that a hero and a villain, or at least two opposing forces, are good for a play, the beginner runs into the phrase "unity of opposites" as a recipe for preventing the antagonists from quitting in the middle of the drama. "Unity of opposites" is intended to mean that the antagonists are so opposite in every way that they can't possibly get together.

A word that would seem to have little chance of being misunderstood or distorted is "exposition"; obviously it would seem to refer to things out of the past that have to be explained to the audience at some point in the play. Yet one writer gets hold of a dictionary and a thesaurus, and decides that the word means "the act of exposing," with the result that he thinks exposition deals with practically everything, including the meaning of the play, the plot, the characters and their background, the atmosphere, the mood, even the scenery. Just to make things a little more confusing, the writer says: "What most teachers call exposition, we prefer to call 'point of attack.' "

"Rising Action," "Premise," and "Proposition"

Another source of confusion lies in the terms "rising action" and "falling action." Gustav Freytag, the first man to diagram the action of a play, followed Aristotle and divided a play into two equal parts with the crisis in the middle, thus producing the profile of a pyramid. To arrive at this he confined the rising action to the exertion of the will or desires of the hero; he called the crisis the point where the hero's will runs into the challenge of the opposing force; and he defined the falling action as the resulting descent to a tragic conclusion. Thompson points out that Freytag's analysis of a tragedy, if applied to *Hamlet,* would place the point of the pyramid in the scene where Hamlet spares the king at his prayers. We still use Freytag's terms, but we give them a new meaning. Rising action includes all the mounting excitement of the play up to whatever you call the major crisis, climax, or turning point, and the descending action goes for the rest. Thus the rising action always includes at least two-thirds of a play, generally three-quarters or more, and, in the case of *Hamlet* and many other dramas, all but the last few lines.

Another confusing term is "premise." We usually agree with the dictionaries that its common meaning is a proposition that we accept as the beginning of a line of thought or an argument, and that may lead to the acceptance of another proposition. One writer, however, uses "premise" as if it meant "purpose," and says it includes ideas like "theme," "thesis," "goal," "aim," "driving force," "subject," "plan," "plot," and "basic emotion." And, with all that to go on, he says, "You must have a premise for your play." Finally he boils all plays down to short sentences which he calls premises, and finds that each one has a noun "which suggests character," a verb suggesting action, and a third part which "suggests the end of the play." Thus, the premise of *Juno and the Paycock* is "shiftlessness leads to ruin," of *Dead End,* "poverty encourages crime," and so forth and so on. I suppose it is merely a harmless little exercise in the manufacture of bromides, for the writer admits that you can either start with a premise or discover you've got one in the end, and that neither the premise nor any other part of the play has a life of its own. All it amounts to is saying that a good play will have a moral message.

W. T. Price came forth with a new word in his book *The Analysis of Play Construction and Dramatic Principle,* published in 1908. The word was "proposition." It was "the brief, logical statement or syllogism of that which has to be demonstrated by the complete action of the play." On the surface "proposition" looks like "premise," but it goes a little further as an analysis of the dramatic action in a play. Price has three sections to his proposition, and in them he tells us something about what the characters are really up to. Here is *Hamlet:*

CONDITIONS OF THE ACTION: Hamlet, hearing that his Uncle killed his Father, takes solemn oath to avenge his Father's death, but requires material proof of his Uncle's guilt.

CAUSE OF THE ACTION: The Uncle commits himself in a situation contrived by Hamlet to trap him.

RESULT OF THE ACTION: Will Hamlet, having received proof of his Uncle's guilt, fulfill his vow to avenge his father?

To Price and to his disciple Arthur Edwin Krows the proposition was only a forward step to the plot.

The poor student puts his thumb into the pie of

playwriting theories and comes up with words like "empathy" for identifying yourself with a character, "collision factor" for something that upsets the equilibrium of the hero at the start of the play, "orchestration of characters" for having enough different kinds of people to tell your story effectively, "identification" vs. "detachment" as a distinction between drama and comedy, "drame" for "all non-comic plays the effectiveness of which depends on rousing strong identification," "retardation" for milking a scene, "dilemma" for the result of opposing forces. Then there is the Aristotelian word πεζιπετεῖα, or "peripeteia," which reposed for centuries beneath a headstone reading: "A reversal of fortune that leads to an unexpected conclusion, usually from prosperity to adversity." The quiet of the grave has been disturbed only occasionally; Archer dug up the body in 1912 and called it "peripety," and, lately, a writer mistook the corpse for "suspense," and rechristened it "peripetia."

There are words and phrases that sound as silly as some I have mentioned, but that make more sense, such as Samuel Selden's "Fighting Triad." It is another analytic triptych; there is the "principal force," the "opposing force," and the "deciding agent." For *Romeo and Juliet* this means:

PRINCIPAL FORCE	OPPOSING FORCE	DECIDING FORCE
The passionate desire of a boy and girl to get together	The blind desire of their families to keep them apart.	The power of the boy and girl's love.

Seven Basic Words and Some Definitions

As for the words I myself intend to use, I hope you will not find them too confusing or complicated:

EXPOSITION: Things out of the past that the audience needs to know in order to understand the characters and the plot.

PREPARATION: Things out of the past or the present that have to be planted well ahead of where they will be useful in making a scene or a character plausible or effective.

COMPLICATION: A fact or a character, already planted in the play, which is brought forward to spur the plot into mounting suspense.

SUSPENSE: Worry over the possibility of a conflict and over its outcome.

CONFLICT: A tension between two or more characters that leads to a minor crisis and/or to a major crisis and a climax.

CRISIS: A minor or major development of a conflict.

CLIMAX: The highest point of a series of crises.

Now for some definitions of play structure as a whole. They will do you no harm if you look at them critically and remember something from Finch's *How to Write a Play:*

In a world of art in which every fine play differs in form and content from all other plays, in which the same dramatic material, filtered and resolved by the vision and imagination of a dozen playwrights, may result in a dozen different plays, all good, all true, and all different—in such a world it would be temerity indeed to say, "This is right and that is wrong. This is good, that is bad. Emulate this, avoid that."

There are quite a number of short statements about the nature of a play that are merely truisms and do very little good:

The only valid definition of the dramatic is: any representation which is capable of interesting an average audience in the theatre.— William Archer.

I think there is but one rule that you must always follow —to grip your audience's interest and not to loosen that grip.—Roi Cooper Megrue.

The only absolute rule of playwriting is that you must keep your audience interested. And following a good play structure is the surest way of obeying that rule.—Alan Thompson.

Definitions of Dramatic Structure

How do you achieve a good play structure to keep an audience interested? Now we are in for definitions, and Aristotle began the game. The following is a free combination of the translations of Buckley and Butcher:

Tragedy is an imitation of an action that is serious, complete, and of a certain magnitude, in pleasing language, using each kind of artistic ornament, . . . [conveyed] by men acting and not through narration, and effecting through pity and fear the proper purgation of these emotions.

Here is a modern definition by Rowe of what he calls a plot:

> . . . a series of events of a kind and so arranged as to arrest our attention and hold our interest by creating and maintaining suspense. What is necessary to creation of suspense is conflict, an opposition between two forces, with the outcome uncertain. To be a good conflict, it must be between forces that are well-matched, but not equal. . . . The source of the conflict must contain enough complications to keep the story going, to keep up suspense. . . .

Next there is the matter of unity. As Rowe says:

> In the conflict must be found the first principle of a drama, its unity. A dramatic story is not just a sequence of events . . . unified conflict [is] the basis of drama.

Many theorists dogmatize too much about the conflict of wills, of protagonist and antagonist, of hero and villain, of objective and obstacle. Brunetière was freethinking enough, but he clung to the conflict of wills as the one essential. "Evidently all these alleged Rules effect or express only the most superficial characteristics of the drama. . . . Drama is drama with them or without them. They are only devices which may at any time give place to others. It all depends on the subject, the author, and the public." But further along in his *The Law of the Drama* he pulled out his own iron-clad definition, his own immutable rule:

> The general law of the theatre is defined by the action of a will conscious of itself; and the dramatic species are distinguished by the nature of the obstacles encountered by that will.

Miss Gallaway trails along with Brunetière, but goes a little further in describing the end of a drama:

> First, the common denominator, the universal factor which moves audiences, is not thought, not unpurposive activity, not the mere writing of passion, but will, the effort of an individual to assert his individuality and to find his own harmonious place in his milieu through such an assertion. Second, the action by which he tries to do this is a dramatic action. Third, the playwright's end product, a dramatic climax, is an intense experience of satisfaction for the audience in the final establishment on stage of a harmony broken or threatened during the play.

Frankly, I am baffled by Hegel, whom John Howard Lawson, Egri, and Miss Gallaway swear by. He built a dramatic law out of his dialectic—which is that an initial "thesis," or state of affairs, must inevitably meet its "antithesis," or opposite, that after the conflict the two will merge in a "synthesis," and that this synthesis, as a new "thesis," will meet a new "antithesis," and so on and so on. Hegel believed that "the end and content of an action is only dynamic by reason of the fact that . . . it calls into being in other individuals other objects and passions opposed to it." It is true that "contradiction is the power that moves things," and that, as Lawson interprets Hegel's thought, "action is driven forward by the unstable equilibrium between man's will and his environment—the wills of other men, the forces of society and of nature." But is all this any more than saying that, if a playwright is able to create a dynamic hero, a hero instinct with will, he will have to find or develop or imagine the right kind of antagonist—along with all the clever devices by which they are thrown from one crisis into another and a bigger one?

Maxwell Anderson, discouraged as much by the wilfulness of success as by the reality of failure, sought and found what he thinks is a recipe for good playwriting. "So far as I could make out," he writes, "every new play was a new problem, and the old rules were inapplicable." Here is the solution he found, the magic elixir for long life in a play:

> . . . the mainspring in the mechanism of a modern play is almost invariably a discovery by the hero of some element in his environment or in his own soul of which he has not been aware—or which he has not taken sufficiently into account. . . . A play should lead up to and away from a central crisis, and this crisis should consist in a discovery by the leading character which has an indelible effect on his thought and emotion and completely alters his course of action. The leading character, let me say again,

must make the discovery; it must affect him emotionally; and it must alter his direction in the play.

Anderson's is a sound, basic point. The only problem is to find an interesting leading character and a significant thing for him to discover, and then to work out all the details of action and complication and suspense by which the audience is led up to and away from the central crisis in which the hero makes his all-important —and, of course, it must be dramatic—discovery.

Another poet-dramatist, T. S. Eliot, supplies another recipe for drama: "I tried to keep in mind that in a play, from time to time, something should happen; that the audience should be kept in constant expectation that something is going to happen; and that, when it does happen, it should be different, but not too different, from what the audience had been led to expect."

Behind all the definitions I have cited lies a very simple fact. A play lives by suspense. We go to the theatre to worry. Whether we see a tragedy, a serious drama, or a comedy, we enjoy it fully only if we are made to worry about the outcome of individual scenes and of the play as a whole. Frank Craven, successful playwright as well as actor, said: "Get 'em in hot water and get 'em out again." If it is a comedy, boy meets girl, boy loses girl, and boy gets girl. If it is a tragedy—*Romeo and Juliet,* for example—boy meets girl, boy gets girl, boy loses girl. For "boy" and "girl" you have only to substitute other characters or values, and keep on worrying.

Complication—to Crisis and Suspense

Of course, you are still no nearer to a recipe for making an audience worry through the whole course of a play. After Miss Gallaway repeats her dictum that opposing wills make drama through "the pursuit of a strongly desirable objective by a protagonist who has chances to succeed against a powerful antagonist," she mentions the most important device for keeping the audience worrying and building suspense higher and higher: "[the] course of action is made somewhat devious by a number of complications," and she gives a chapter to the subject. Rowe, too, sees the importance of complications: "They are the stuff of which the bulk of the drama structurally is built." But I think it is quite remarkable that most teachers of playwriting give so little attention to the question of how to create and organize complications; for they recognize that the essence of a play is mounting suspense—which, I believe, only continued complications can produce.

Critics see that no one crisis in a conflict can produce a single climax that will make a satisfactory play. They recognize that there must be many crises and many small climaxes. Yet even Archer, who saw clearly that "the drama may be called the art of crises, as fiction is the art of gradual developments," gave very little attention to how those crises may be multiplied. Henry Arthur Jones, a leading English playwright of fifty years ago, saw the essential need of suspense piled on suspense when he defined a play as "a succession of suspenses and crises, or as a succession of conflicts impending and conflicts raging, carried on in ascending and accelerated climaxes from the beginning to the end of a connected scheme." The problem is how to do this, and the means are complications.

3

The First Problem—Your Material

To act with a purpose is what raises man above the brutes; to invent with a purpose, to imitate with a purpose, is what distinguishes genius from the petty artists who only invent to invent, imitate to imitate.

LESSING

The Test of Material

NOW FOR THE OBVIOUS. YOUR PLAY CAN NEVER BE better than its material—its characters and what they feel and think and do. Your material must be worth the effort that goes into playmaking. It must be significant and provocative enough to interest thousands upon thousands of your fellow beings. It must be of the kind that fits the peculiar demands of the theatre. Your material must not only permit the building up of conflict and suspense; ideally it should be capable of *generating* conflict and suspense with the least amount of conscious contrivance on your part and without the danger of distorting and falsifying character. Only the perfection of craftsmanship—and the beginning playwright is incapable of such perfection—can make poor material effective; craftsmanship can never make it significant and compelling. Though the adroit but shallow play may be an immediate success, in a very few years it will be properly forgotten. In *Merrily We Roll Along*, George S. Kaufman and Moss Hart have one of their characters say to a writer of skillful but unimportant plays: ". . . the trouble with the plays you're doing is you don't dare stop. You've got to write one a year, or they'll forget you ever wrote a line. But you write one good play, and they'll always know who you are."

It is possible to devote the larger part of a book to the problem of where to find material. Samson Raphaelson has virtually done this in his *The Natural History of Playwriting*. In this transcript of class discussions at the University of Illinois, he develops a single basic point with which almost everyone agrees. Until you have had five or six years of experience outside academic walls—or a reasonable facsimile thereof—and have done considerable playwriting, you must look for your material close around you. If you have grown up on an Iowa farm or in a small Middle Western city, don't write about Park Avenue in New York or Chinatown in San Francisco. Instead, deal with people and events that you know at first-hand. And, knowing your material, you must still approach it and develop it with an honesty and a sincerity equal to or exceeding your skill as a craftsman.

If Familiarity Breeds Respect . . .

If you know the personal life of a playwright, you can see that when he wrote sincerely of people he knew at first-hand he was successful, and you can also see that he floundered and failed when he tried to use material with which he was unfamiliar or to use familiar material that he did not respect. O'Neill is an excellent example. From 1913, when he was twenty-four, through 1916 he wrote at least thirteen one-act plays and five long plays. A few of the short plays dealt with the sea—which he had followed off and on for two years as a sailor before the mast—but, except for one, they were inept and theatrical. Again with one exception, the rest of the plays, long and short, were no better, and the exception, *Before Breakfast,* was only a Grand Guignol *tour de force* in which a nagging wife addressed a monologue to her husband in the off-stage bathroom, and he cut his throat at the curtain. In the other short play that distinguished his first four years of playwriting, *Bound East for Cardiff,* O'Neill dealt successfully for the first time with the rich material he had gathered in his many months at sea. It was three years, however, after the writing of this play before he began to work steadily and successfully the mine of his own deep and special experience, and to produce in *Ile, In the Zone, The Long Voyage Home,* and *The Moon of the Caribbees* drama that set him firmly on the road to artistic and ultimately commercial success. Soon, in *The Rope* and *Beyond the Horizon,* he began to use familiar New England characters. *Anna Christie* and *The Straw* came out of first-hand experience with waterfront people and life in a sanitarium for the tubercular. There were failures in this period, of course, but much more of steady progress. After the experiment of *The Emperor Jones*—which came out of a trip to Central America—O'Neill was ready to try his hand at expressionism and masks and asides, and to use his imagination in plays that were either out of our time, like *Marco Millions,* or that translated into another time mythical figures like those in *Mourning Becomes Electra.*

Ibsen—who began as a poet but was fortunate enough to work in a theatre as director, manager, and designer from the age of twenty-three to twenty-eight—started with a blank-verse drama on the Roman Catiline and spent a number of years transferring to the stage the history, myths, and sagas of Scandinavia before, at thirty-four, he turned to his own time, and haltingly wrote *Love's Comedy* in 1862. He then moved ahead past *Brand* and *Peer Gynt* and *The League of Youth* to his mastery—indeed, creation—of modern social realism through *A Doll's House* in 1879, when he was already fifty-one.

"The greatest mistake I made as a young fellow," says Raphaelson, "a mistake that is made by all but lucky and exceptionally clear-headed writers, was placing too much importance on the art of invention.

. . . The world is oversupplied with people who can think up things. But looking at yourself, looking at people, getting a viewpoint on them that clarifies them, gives them meaning, and expressing that viewpoint in a form—that is the highest of arts."

With plenty of time for research, a graduate student could write a very bulky dissertation on how far the success and the failure of the early plays of well-known dramatists have turned, not so much on their innate abilities as on their familiarity or lack of familiarity with their materials. Along the way, to be sure, he would come upon examples of young playwrights of unusual talent who have had momentary but not enduring success by dealing skillfully with people and things outside their lives. Such a man was Edward Sheldon, star-student of Baker's early classes at Harvard and author of *Romance*, which ran for years in New York and London. While still at Harvard, Sheldon saw a play of his, *Salvation Nell*, produced with success by Mrs. Fiske; a year later (1909) came *The Nigger* at the New Theatre, the first and only American play staged by this institution endowed for repertory by the rich of New York; in 1911 Mrs. Fiske successfully produced *The Boss.* These plays were effective in a day when, as O'Neill has said with only slight exaggeration, "a play of any originality or integrity was automatically barred from a hearing in our theatre." If Sheldon, as well-fixed as he was well-read, had written of what he knew by contact rather than of slum characters, the racial problem in the South, and ward politics, the plays might not have won success or even been produced at the time, but they might now be in the repertory of the community and university producing groups that form our national theatre.

Among Baker's early students was Frederick H. Koch, who began to teach playwriting in North Dakota and went on to found the Carolina Playmakers at the University of North Carolina. He—along with many later teachers—urged his pupils to write about the people of their own communities or states, as the Abbey Theatre in Dublin had encouraged new playwrights to deal with the Irish peasant and the Irish slum-dweller. Koch found no Synge or O'Casey, but he developed Paul Green, and his Carolina Playmakers produced many a salty and refreshing comedy of the Piedmont and the Appalachians, and dramas, too.

In a large university a student seldom has any personal contact with folk-life or slum-life, but he knows how his own generation and class live in the city or the home town. I have seen young playwrights find excellent material in the fellow-students of a sorority and a fraternity, in an unmarried aunt with a somewhat pixilated brother and sister to care for, in middle-class families of small towns, in a sophisticated and neurotic woman of Beverly Hills. I have known veterans who dealt effectively with the things they encountered overseas during the war. I have seen a GI transfer successfully to the Balkans—where he had never been—the ruthless conflict of Fascism and Communist ideologies and violences that he had encountered here and in the service; while, in the same class, I found a student who translated to the stage all too literally and therefore dully what had happened to him, and what he had seen around him, when he had been thrown into the "drunk tank" of a suburban jail for a traffic violation.

Distillation of Character

Though the student should begin by writing of things at first-hand, he should avoid for some time the thing that is nearest to him—himself. Don't make your personality and your dilemmas the center of a play until you are sure you can apply as much interpretive understanding and imagination to your own character as you can apply—and apply so much more easily—to your acquaintances. Almost all the people you meet and know—whether you know them deeply or superficially—must be changed, amplified, developed, twisted this way or that, to make them more interesting and more useful. You must put them through a kind of distillation process before they can fit your dramatic ends or seem as real and as significant as they should be. This process of distillation is even more essential if you deal with yourself—and much more difficult. Raphaelson notes that once, when he found himself having trouble with a character because it was too nearly a portrait of himself, he solved the problem by exaggerating the qualities in himself that he dislikes, and making the character a "heel."

O'Neill was thirty before he began to make partial and tentative ventures at self-interpretation in *Beyond the Horizon* and *The Straw.* At thirty-five he blundered as he tried too literal a self-interpretation in *Welded.* By greater distillation he made *The Great God Brown* a brilliant play. Looking back at his youth, he achieved a fine folk-comedy in *Ah, Wilderness!*

A playwright needs some years of practice in his art and some years of experience of life before he is ready to move along from what he has seen and experienced at first-hand to what he may read about, imagine, and interpret. Yet even then it is his experience and his personality that provide the stimulus to create and the critical judgment to interpret and to shape alien matter into good drama. The dramatic process remains personal and dependent on experience, but, as a writer matures, the area of the material he can master expands with his expanding personality and experience.

Imaginative Creation

Robert Ardrey once gave a class of mine an illuminating account of how experience, reading, and maturity worked together in creating *Thunder Rock.* The characters, the dramatic idea, and the plot in general outline came to him while he sat bored for twenty minutes at a performance of the ballet *Les Sylphides.* It was at a time, shortly after Munich, when he was much concerned with the problem of a civilized man in a world that seemed headed for barbarism. Could such a man escape action or responsibility? How would he try? And what would show him that he had to live in the world about him? For a place of escape, Ardrey's mind went back to a lighthouse on Nantucket Island, where he had spent the summer of the Czech crisis under its sweeping beacon. Here was the perfect ivory tower; but, to make it still more perfect, he moved it as near as possible to the center of the United States by putting it on an island in Lake Michigan. Then he remembered stories he had heard as a young Chicagoan of the foundering of many a passenger ship on that inland sea. Such a boat could bring the world to his hero. To find the right world, the world that would force the escapist back sharply to the reality of the struggle between Nazism and democracy, Ardrey recalled from his reading the refugees that fled from German and Austrian reaction in 1848. He put these people on a ship and wrecked them on the rock where his ivory tower stood. But, in order to make the issue a real one of today and to increase the vitality of the spiritual problem faced by his hero, he made the time of the drama 1939 while the ship remained a ship of a hundred years ago, gone to the bottom with all its crew and passengers. Ardrey's hero, unable to live by and with and of himself alone, summoned back the dead—first the captain, then some of the men and women, together with the problems they had faced in the Old World. As the captain became more and more real in the mind of the hero, the captain and his passengers began to take on a life of their own, uncontrolled by the man in the ivory tower. At the end of the play, as a result of what he had seen of the refugees of '48—all a figment of his imagination, playing upon the reality of today—the man left his ivory tower to fight again for a freer and a better world. This is imaginative creation, only half out of experience. It goes a step further than *The Emperor Jones*, which O'Neill made out of the terrors of jungle and jungle noises that he felt when he was sick with malaria in Honduras, and what a circus man told him about President Sam of Haiti and his silver bullet.

Obviously you must find characters in the life about you; they are one of the basic materials of playwriting, and, generally speaking, the most important. But there is also the matter of plots. Where do you find them?

Characters Can Make Plots

"There are no plots in nature," says Alan Thompson, and he is measurably right. Characters there are in nature; a great many of them require little alteration for use in a play. There are many situations in real life, too, but few plots if any. You may come upon a ready-made one, but that is unlikely. Those that do exist are in rudimentary form, badly organized, incomplete. They must be made over, added to, and reshaped for dramatic effectiveness.

Plots are usually found in characters. A plot may spring from a single individual whose nature suggests conflict when placed in a particular social setting, or from two or more dynamically different characters. You may develop a plot from a situation that you have come across or heard of, plus certain characters that you know or develop. A mood or a background may suggest a plot, but you will work hard developing a story of this sort, and, again, the selection of characters will play a most important part. A plot based on a theme may be easier, if it doesn't run to propaganda.

A couple of years ago a student suggested the oddest source of plots I have ever come across, and the most absurd. He had told me three or four very bad ones, and I had suggested that it might be a good idea if he dropped the course. He answered: "Please give me a few days. When I have a title I can always get a plot out of it, and a friend has promised to give me a lot of titles on Thursday."

What Price "Originality," Morbidity, and Speed

For three centuries our theatre has placed a violent and, perhaps, undue emphasis on originality of plot. Originality was unknown to the writers of Greek tragedy. Indeed they were required by tradition to rework the stories—along with the characters—of Greek religion, myth, or history. Most of their dramas dealt with one of two families, the house of Atreus of Mycenae and that of Laius of Thebes. Shakespeare led the Elizabethans in the adaptation of old romances or old plays or history; only two of his main-plots have not been traced to older sources, and the plays based on them, *The Merry Wives of Windsor* and *Love's Labour's Lost,* are not his best.

While crying for originality and berating playwrights for stealing plots, we have not enjoyed quite so much novelty of plot as we carelessly suppose. In spite of Polti, there are more than thirty-six plots, but not an unlimited number. Many have been used over and over again, and rightly; for novelty is a questionable virtue compared with the other values in a play. The plot of Eugene O'Neill's *Desire Under the Elms* is strikingly like that of Sidney Howard's *They Knew What They Wanted.* An old man on a farm marries a young woman from far away, whom he doesn't know. The new wife has an affair with a young man in the house—in Howard's play a hired man, in O'Neill's the old man's son. A baby is on the way. Yet, for all this close resemblance in plot, the two plays are utterly different. The characters are different. The mood is different. The end is different. One is a tragedy, one a comedy. Each is unique. In a later play, *Mourning Becomes Electra,* O'Neill proved how unimportant originality of plot can be by going back to the story of the house of Atreus.

The apprentice playwright has a tendency toward tragedy, rather than comedy. The serious play, whether tragic or not, seems easier to write. He sometimes has also an unfortunate leaning toward the painful. His interest in the tragic and the painful sometimes leads him into the gruesome and the horrible. He mistakenly sees in the macabre and the distressing something that is powerful and effective. It is not. The story of the depraved man who preys on helpless and befuddled old ladies, of the murderer reveling in the cruel and horrifying ingenuities of John Collier's short stories, is not rewarding material for the theatre. Such stuff is for the study. It is too torturous for common contemplation in a crowded auditorium. The "cat and mouse" drama may have a success of curiosity at times, but nothing more. Usually it achieves only complete and immediate failure.

Avoid the tragedy of frustration. "The first job the playwright has in the theatre," writes Howard Lindsay, "is to engage the emotions of the audience favorably toward one or more of the characters. . . . The play that ends in mere frustration for the people in whom the audience is emotionally interested will not satisfy them, for frustration is one of the most unhappy experiences in our lives." Tragedy is satisfying only when the greatness of the victim becomes manifest in his death or defeat, or when his downfall leaves some sense of accomplishment behind it.

Among the things that the apprentice must guard against is speed—speed of conception and speed of work. Rowe has written: "The thought that comes most easily is most likely to have come to many other minds." He might have cautioned you against the thought that comes most easily *and most simply*. Because there are no new plots and not too many old ones, greater importance attaches to the characterization behind and within the plot, the mood or background, new relationships of old elements, any one of a number of factors that bring a plot to life and make it seem fresher and more effective. It is in the assembling and combination of a lot of elements—most of them old or familiar—that you create an effect of freshness, even spontaneity. And such work takes time.

Speed of writing is dangerous, too. A play is too intricate a thing to be built up quickly and easily even in outline. The choice of characters, their effect on each other, the order of scenes, the introduction of new factors, new complications—all these and many other things take time to work out. They take time not just because they are numerous, but because each factor affects the others, and some one of them may surprise you by violently upsetting what you have planned.

When you have your scenario in order and you think you have only the dialogue to write, you will find plenty of tedious and baffling work ahead of you. As the characters begin to speak, they often seem to get ideas of their own. They develop new situations and upset old ones. Even if they prove docile, and the outline of your play holds true, you have still a lot of labor ahead of you—unless you have an amazing flair for dialogue. Lord Dunsany says he wrote *A Night at an Inn* "between tea and dinner," but I should guess that Synge did not toss off *Riders to the Sea* at any such breakneck speed. Arthur Schnitzler, the most careful of craftsmen, jotted down dramatic characters, themes, and plots as they occurred to him, put them away for consideration, took them out after many months or even years, developed them in detail, and put them away again for later development and revision. On some of his plays he spent ten, twenty, or even thirty years—another and extreme demonstration of the old truism that plays are not written but rewritten.

How to Start a Play

You can read, if you want to, a lot of very confusing statements about how to start a play or find a plot. Some are simple, like Rowe's: "All that is necessary as a starting point is an incident which precipitates conflict, an incident which makes the turning point or crisis of a conflict, or an incident which resolves a conflict," but you may still be left wondering how to recognize such an incident and how to carry on from there. Archer simplified the matter by dreaming the plot of *The Green Goddess* one night. He confessed, some years earlier, that he "occupied several hours of a long country walk in, as I believed, creating out of nothing at all a dramatic story. When at last I modeled it into some sort of coherency . . . I found I had re-invented *Hedda Gabler*." Archer recommended "the plot that chooses us . . . the idea which comes when we least expect it, perhaps from the most unlikely quarter, clamours at the gates of birth, and will not let us rest till it be clothed in dramatic flesh and blood." I have seen a play start with a mere description of a set of characters. The student's *dramatis personae* were so real, so vivid, so vital, so well observed during a stretch in the Pentagon Building in the last war that they almost wrote the play for him.

In a newspaper interview, that exceptionally able playwright Lillian Hellman gives us an interesting insight into the primary workings of a dramatist's mind:

> The evolution of *Watch on the Rhine* is quite involved and, I'm afraid, not very interesting. When I was working on *The Little Foxes* I hit on the idea—well, there's a small Midwestern American town, average or perhaps a little more isolated than average, and into that town Europe walks in the form of a titled couple—a pair of titled Europeans—pausing on their way to the West Coast. I was quite excited, thought of shelving *The Foxes* to work on it. But when I did get to it I couldn't get it moving. It started all right—and then stuck.

Later I had another idea. What would be the reactions of some sensitive people who had spent much of their lives starving in Europe and found themselves as house guests in the home of some very wealthy Americans? What would they make of all the furious rushing around, the sleeping tablets taken when there is no time to sleep them off, the wonderful dinners ordered and never eaten, and so on and so on. . . . That play didn't work either. I kept worrying at it, and the earlier people, the titled couple, returned continually. It would take all afternoon and probably a lot of tomorrow to trail all the steps that made those two plays into *Watch on the Rhine*. The titled couple are still in, but as minor characters. The Americans are nice people, and so on. All is changed, but the new play grew out of the other two.

Sometimes two incidents or story elements, remote from each other in time and place, can be combined to make effective story material. In writing the film, *Young Mr. Lincoln,* Lamar Trotti used a trial that he had once covered as a young reporter in Georgia, in which two brothers were accused of murder. He slid this back a hundred years and made it the law case that Lincoln won by proving, through an *Old Farmer's Almanac,* that there was no moon on the night when a witness for the prosecution claimed to have identified a murderer because the scene of struggle in a clearing in the woods was "moon bright."

A bad way to start a play is to have what beginners call "an idea"—some striking or bizarre situation devoid of character and so limited in human appeal that is good for no more than an ironic paragraph or a very short short story. Dunsany confesses that such an idea —a king clothed in rags, sitting upon the ground gnawing a bone, and vastly enjoying it—was the basis of his *Argimenes and the Unknown Warrior.* As he recognized later—and much too late—from that situation the play ran downhill and ended in superficiality.

The "Theme Play"

Along with the instinct to imitate, the human animal—particularly the writer—has an instinct "to say something," to convey a meaning, even a message. This often leads a playwright to look for a theme or to find one in the people and the incidents that he becomes interested in. A theme may frequently be the inevitable outcome of a dramatic plot, but it is seldom the initial impulse for the writing of a good play. I doubt that Shakespeare began *Romeo and Juliet* with the idea of proving that "great love defies even death," or *Macbeth* with the theme that "ruthless ambition leads to its own destruction." Did Sidney Kingsley write *Dead End* to prove that "poverty encourages crime"? Certainly no playwright ever got very far by deciding to write a play to demonstrate that mothers should love their children or that drink is an evil or prohibition is bad. A bald theme never motivated the writing of a good play. In every good play you can usually find a theme, bald and obvious or deep and potent, but the theme is not what makes the play good. *Macbeth* is not great because someone can read it and say, "Ah, you see, ruthless ambition leads to its own destruction." *Hamlet* defeats such theme-hunting, as critics pointed out to Sir Laurence Olivier when he explained in a foreword to his film that this was "the story of a man who could not make up his mind."

Character and Theme in Ibsen

As Raphaelson says, there is danger in "the method which starts with a theme and then rummages around for characters and a plot to fit it." Ibsen—master of the "theme play" though he was—never worked that way. He had convictions on the "woman question," as it was called seventy-five years ago, but Archer says that *A Doll's House* "was woven from a commonplace story of a woman who forged a check to redecorate her drawing-room," while a Scandinavian authority on Ibsen, Halvdan Koht, says that it all began through the playwright's acquaintance with a married woman whom he called "the lark" and whose marriage seemed like "a doll's house." According to Koht, before Ibsen wrote his play he heard that "the husband became ill; his wife had to earn money, and without her husband's knowledge she contracted debts. When he found it out he became angry, and the thing brought about a crisis in their married life. It affected her so strongly that she had to go to a nerve clinic." As a matter of fact, in

The League of Youth, written ten years before, Ibsen had a character who burst forth: "You have dressed me up like a doll. You have played with me as you have played with a child. Oh, what a joy it would have been to take a share in your burdens!" Here was the germ of *A Doll's House.*

Whether or not Ibsen wrote his great realistic dramas to prove theses, when he was done he had certainly presented themes. Today some of those themes seem what painters call old hat. H. L. Mencken, having examined Ibsen's plays "in the privacy of my sacristy," got much antic pleasure in writing of Ibsen's plays: "What I found in them was simply a vast mass of hollow platitudes—that a woman of any intelligence, treated like a doll by her husband, does not like it; that a man suffering from what was then called a social disease runs some risk of having cuckoo children; that becoming a mother, to a woman who hates her husband, is extremely unpleasant, and so on and so on."

If ideas like these—needed as they were in Ibsen's era—had been all that he had to offer, his plays would not live as they do today. We may still approve their themes or we may take them as obvious old truisms, but we see the plays with pleasure because of the firm characterizations and the skill in dramaturgy that Ibsen lavished on them. His themes bother us no more than his swallowing and then regurgitating through the mouth of Helmar in *A Doll's House* the theory that

thievery and extravagance are hereditary. (Today he would haul out "conditioning" instead, and Helmar would say that the example of Nora's father had taught her those two vices.) Ibsen's best plays are still powerful after sixty or seventy years, but not because, as Alan Thompson puts it, "He perfected the constructive artifices of the 'well-made play' to such a point that they became fine art." Rather, as W. A. Darlington writes, they "are alive today because when it came to the point Ibsen always sank the social reformer in the dramatist, and put his story and his characters before the lesson they were designed to teach."

The nineties and the early years of the twentieth century were cursed with a peculiar offspring of the kind of drama that Ibsen originated. This was the so-called "problem-play" of popular playwrights like Arthur Wing Pinero, author of *The Second Mrs. Tanqueray.* They dealt mostly with the "eternal triangle" in one form or another. A writer in *The New Republic* in 1918 described the "queer artificiality of the problems they asked us to look at. Is it a good plan, on the whole, to leave your uncongenial wife in London and go traveling in Italy with another lady who happens to be a stump-speaking rebel? Is he a wise widower who marries several men's mistress and bets against his daughter's falling in love with one of his second wife's ex-lovers?" Playwrights of more sincerity and stature, such as Eugene Brieux and John Galsworthy, dealt with realer problems, matters like syphilis, unwanted motherhood, industrial strife, and the injustice of justice.

Perhaps it is safest to say that a good playwright starts with an attitude rather than a theme—an attitude toward certain characters or a certain aspect of life.

Beware of the Propaganda Play

Theme may be almost inevitable in the "serious drama" for which Diderot, the French encyclopedist and playwright, called aloud when the stage was given over exclusively to either tragedy or comedy. The fact that the serious drama began to take form in the latter part of the nineteenth century as the evils of uncontrolled capitalism grew obvious, led its playwrights toward what we now call "social significance." This did not necessarily mean the birth of the propaganda play; here in America, between the time of Diderot and of Brieux, we had had anti-British plays and anti-slavery plays. The difference between the propaganda play and what has been called social drama is that the propaganda play deliberately proposes a general solution, while, as someone has pointed out, in social drama the solution of the general problem is personal.

"If you *are* going to write what is called a propaganda play," says Howard Lindsay, "don't let any character in the play know what the propaganda is. Act it out. Don't talk it out. The minute you let one of your characters know what the propaganda is that you are trying to put across, that character will start talking, you can't stop him, and your play will become self-conscious."

In *How's Your Second Act?* Arthur Hopkins had wise words for the beginning playwright who is rash enough to try deliberately for social significance through a preconceived theme; "In the theatre, I do not want the emotion that arises out of thought, but thought that arises out of emotion." To create an emotional reaction in his audience is the first job of the playwright. Theme may—and probably will—follow.

Which brings us back to the all-important and inescapable fact that content—content of character and content of emotion, properly suited to dramatic development—is the basis of a good and potentially effective play. Your material comes first. But you must know something of how a play is effectively put together before you can judge and use your material.

4

The Power of Character

> The strictest observation of the rules cannot outweigh the smallest fault in a character.
>
> LESSING

If You Can Create Characters . . .

WILLIAM ARCHER, AS VIGOROUS A PARTISAN OF CHARacter as Lessing, once wrote, "No teaching or study can enable a man . . . to observe and portray human character. . . . Specific directions for character-drawing would be like rules for becoming six feet high. Either you have it in you or you have it not." "The power to observe, penetrate, and reproduce character," he concluded, "cannot be acquired."

It is nevertheless true that, if a writer has a talent for character, criticism can aid him in developing it. By pointing out stereotypes, by showing him why certain characters are unbelievable, by urging him to elaborate and enrich the people of his play, the teacher can eliminate faults and spur the student on to deeper observation and ampler expression. Conceding that "characterization is something that cannot be taught or learned," Rowe asserts in *Write That Play:* "It can, however, be cultivated, and there are a few principles which give assistance in its application to drama."

In my opinion there are three such principles, and the first of these is that all the characters of a play must be believable. They must be believable in themselves and they must be consistent in their behavior and reactions. If the audience does not believe that a character whom it has come to know would behave as the author makes him behave, if the audience won't accept the reaction of the character to a situation, then any scene that is an outgrowth of his reaction will seem false and implausible. Indeed, the author may never be able to re-establish the emotional confidence of the audience in his entire play.

The next principle is that the important figures in a play must be rich in characterization. They must have many facets to their personalities, many interests, enthusiasms, and sympathies or prejudices, all reaching into the past. This will not only make them more interesting as people, but it will also provide more possibilities for emotional reactions, and emotional reactions make for conflict and suspense. In comedy, perhaps, richness of characterization may not be so important, but where there are stereotypes—as sometimes in Molière—comedy verges on farce.

In the third place, the characters must be so selected and developed that they include people who are bound to react upon each other, bound to clash, as well as lesser characters who by intervening will heighten the clash or perhaps help finally to resolve it.

In Spite of Aristotle

The importance of characterization has not always been recognized as it is today. Aristotle may be blamed for this, for in his *Poetics* he placed first emphasis upon the action, or plot: "The plot . . . is the first principle, and, as it were, the soul of the tragedy; character holds second place." "Character," he wrote, "comes in as a subsidiary of the action." Aristotle was curiously blind to the development of character in Greek tragedy. He said, truly enough, that "without action, tragedy cannot exist," but, he continued, "it may exist without characters." Now if, instead of writing about tragedy, he had been dealing with melodrama—a form unknown to the Greek theatre of his day—he would have been right. When Archer wrote: "A play can exist without anything that can be called character, but not without some sort of action," the kind of play he had in mind was not high tragedy or serious drama, but merely melodrama or farce—"an ingenious toy, but scarcely a vital work of art."

It is a curious thing that the astute Aristotle should thus have overemphasized the importance of plot as against character, for the Greek tragedies prove him wrong. Both their stories and their characters were strictly prescribed; the playwright had to deal with the events and people of an almost mythological history, and nothing else. In striving for individuality in his work it was the characters that he altered and illuminated, far more than the stories. When a dramatist made a new version of a tragedy, and made it fresher and more exciting by new ways of developing the old plot, he did this largely by changing and improving upon characterization. Aeschylus, Sophocles, and Euripides all wrote plays about Electra, and in each she is measurably different. Turning from Electra as the blind, dogged avenger of the earlier plays, Euripides tried to imagine what sort of woman could live with her hatred for so many years and then work out her vengeance by the murder of her mother; his Electra was a woman who had lived so long between hate and love that at the terrible end she had become a creature of shaken and shattered nerves and desperate fortitude.

Egri in his *The Art of Dramatic Writing* shows that Oedipus, as Sophocles drew him, was a character portrait of a man of definite human traits, and also demonstrates that the character of Oedipus actually shaped—almost created—the action of the play: "If Oedipus had been any other kind of man, tragedy would not have befallen him. Had he not been hot-tempered, he would not have killed a stranger on the road. Had he not been stubborn, he would not have forced the issue of who killed Laius. With rare perseverance he dug out the smallest details, continuing because he was honest, even when the accusing finger pointed at him. Had he not been honest, he would not have punished the murderer by blinding himself." The character of Oedipus was the only possible explanation of the old myth. Character and action were inseparable.

Character Equals Plot

To drive home the vital importance of character and its co-equal status with plot, let me quote seven writers:

"I do not see how plot and character can be regarded separately."—*Marian Gallaway.*

"A plot cannot begin without a character, because plot is character in action."—*Maren Elwood.*

"Action ought to exist for the sake of character . . . the play will be of small account as a work of art unless character, at a very early point, enters into and conditions its development. . . . The difference between a live play and a dead one is that in the former the characters control the plot, while in the latter the plot controls the characters."—*William Archer.*

"The dramatist who hangs his characters to his plot instead of hanging his plot to his characters is guilty of cardinal sins."—*John Galsworthy.*

"Character is the fundamental material we are forced to work with."—*Lajos Egri.*

"Get your characters and they will make your play for you."—*Bronson Howard.*

"Characterization is the content of the play."—*Kenneth T. Rowe.*

The Labor of Characterization

Beyond the talent for recognizing useful, effective characters, fitting them into drama, and bringing them to life, lies an enormous amount of work. "In the two hours of a play," says Miss Gallaway, "the audience must know more about the characters than it learns of most acquaintances in a year." To meet this problem, what means can the playwright employ beyond the inspiration of the moment, sheer imagination meeting each plot emergency as it arises? O'Neill developed the habit of writing out the life stories of his characters with extraordinary fullness before he had completed his plot outline, let alone begun to write dialogue. Of Nora in *A Doll's House,* Ibsen once told a friend: "The things I know about that young woman that aren't in the play would surprise you." Whether he put down on paper much about his characters before he began the actual writing of the script, he has described how his acquaintance with them grew as he wrote the various drafts of his play:

When I am writing I must be alone; if I have eight characters of a drama to do with I have society enough; they keep me busy; I must learn to know them. And this process of making their acquaintance is slow and painful. I make, as a rule, three casts [presumably the translator means different drafts of the play] of my dramas, which differ considerably from each other. I mean in characteristics, not in the course of the treatment. When I first settle down to work out my material, I feel as if I have to get to know my characters on a railway journey; the first acquaintance is struck up, and we have chatted about this and that. When I write it down again, I already see everything much more clearly, and I know the people as if I had stayed with them for a month at a watering place. I have grasped the leading points of their characters and their little peculiarities.

Egri suggests as a guide to the "bone structure" of a character eight items under "physiology" from "sex" to "heredity," nine items under "sociology" from "class" to "amusement, hobbies," and ten items under "psychology" from "sex life, moral standards" to "I.Q."

Characters May Change As You Write

Though you may have studied and developed your characters with immense detail, don't be disturbed if the characters change a bit as you write. You will grow even better acquainted with them as act two follows act one. Characters will affect and develop each other, and sprout traits and attitudes and reactions that you hadn't foreseen. New plot turns may grow from these expansions and changes in characters; they must be examined and appraised, accepted or rejected. "Effective characters," as Krows points out in *Playwriting for Profit*, "must do *everything* of their own volition, and yet cannot be permitted to do *anything* merely because they want to do it." I have heard a number of practiced playwrights describe how a character has started to run away with a play, while another has refused to do what was expected of him in the scenario; they have told me how they have had to make important changes in earlier material because of what they have discovered, too late, about the essential nature of some of their characters. Bronson Howard, a fairly successful playwright of forty and fifty years ago, once said of his characters: "In a measure they are independent of me and my whims." St. John Ervine writes that a playwright may have "no more power to understand his people and to direct their lives with complete success than a parent has to understand the lives of his children or to direct them with complete success. He need not be greatly disturbed if they insist on going their own way. On the contrary, he should feel some elation at this sign of life in them. Docile characters may be dead characters. If an author does not, at some moment in the making of his play, feel his people straining to escape from his control, then he may feel certain that they are too servile to be worth much, or that he has failed to breathe life into their nostrils."

What a Character Can Do to a Plot

Egri has much to say about how the particular nature of a character can affect the course of a play. He describes how the action of *Romeo and Juliet* would have been altered if Shakespeare had cast the brooding Hamlet as the hero instead of the impetuous son of the Montagues. To show how character can dictate plot—which means that a playwright has to choose a particular character for a particular plot, or a plot for a character—Egri analyzes a trite plot in terms of more or less stereotyped characters:

> A husband starts on a two-day trip, but forgets something and comes back to the house. He finds his wife in another man's arms. Let us suppose that the husband is a man of five feet three. The lover is a giant. The situation hinges on the husband—what will he do? If he is free of the author's interference, he will do what his character dictates, what his physical, social, and psychological make-up tell him to do.
>
> If he is a coward, he may apologize, beg forgiveness for his intrusion, and flee—grateful that the lover let him go unmolested.
>
> But perhaps the husband's short stature has made him cocky, has forced him to be aggressive. He springs at the big man in a fury, unmindful that he may be the loser.
>
> Perhaps he is a cynic, and sneers; perhaps he is imperturable, and laughs; perhaps any number of things—depending on the character.

A coward might create a farce, a brave man might create a tragedy.

The Value of Complexity

From Ibsen and Strindberg to Eugene O'Neill and on to Arthur Miller and Tennessee Williams, our best playwrights—and, of late years, some not so good—have tried quite consciously to go beyond simple characterizations to characterizations that are complex, characterizations that involve and invite psychological analysis. It is not enough that a character should be cowardly or aggressive, cynical or imperturbable, if he is Egri's little husband. It is not enough that he should be warm and impetuous, or simple and jealous, or consummately evil—a condensed version, as it were, of Romeo or Othello or Iago. Besides being moody or melancholy—as Hamlet was—he must provide through thought and action—as Hamlet did—an insight into the deeper processes of the conscious and unconscious mind. Characters must be complex instead of simple.

One of Ibsen's simpler contributions to the theatre was a vivid demonstration that a character who is dramatically useful, as well as true to life, is not one unmixed color, black or white, "good" or "bad." In Ibsen's first masterpiece of realism, *A Doll's House,* we find in Nora an impetuous, warm, and child-like woman who has within her the sober depths of her final revolt. We find in Torvald a husband who can be complacent, selfish, and insensitive, and yet kindly, passionate, and in the end desperately disillusioned and even understanding. Characters like Torvald, characters that combine virtues and failings, traits that are admirable and traits that are mean, are for mature audiences in a mature theatre. I remember that when, as a boy in high school, I first saw *A Doll's House,* only a few years after the death of Queen Victoria and the end of the Victorian era, I was carried along by the play up to the last scene—the heart of Ibsen's drama and the heart of his theme—and then, in my immaturity, I could not see why Nora had to shut the door on her life with Torvald. He was a kind husband, and, if he had been a bit selfish and obtuse, he had now seen the error of his ways. I wanted—and expected—Nora and Torvald to live happily together ever after.

The modern playwright has discovered a simpler thing than Ibsen's "good and bad." It is complexity of character *in terms of ornament.* He dwells on details like personal interests and hobbies, things that may or may not have any relation to character or plot. Even the screen writer has learned the trick; of the thieves and murderers in *The Asphalt Jungle,* one is devoted to cats, another dreams of his boyhood farm in Kentucky, the elderly leader is trapped by his monomania for adolescent girls. Shakespeare did something of the same when he made Hamlet a critic and devotee of the actor's art.

Ornamental details may be not very important, but they can sometimes be helpful. If you must have a hero who is a poet, an artist, or a musician—and therefore suspect to the average audience and basically unacceptable—you can make him palatable if you give him little failings, prejudices, and enthusiasms that are common to "average people," if you show that he follows comic strips, admires Al Capp and Li'l Abner, can't get along with his mother-in-law, makes model planes or fishing flies, reads *Esquire* or *The Sporting News,* does common, everyday things that contrast happily and democratically with his higher interests.

The superficial activities of a character can be used to tell something deeper about him. If he reads Proust or builds a television set or collects masks it may be an indication of an inferiority complex and an attempt to compensate for it. The girl who won't use lipstick and who dresses mannishly may have nothing wrong with her morally, but may feel a deep and false sense of her inadequacy as a female. In developing such aspects of character the modern playwright is going back of Freud to Strindberg, who thought in 1887 that audiences were deeply interested in psychological explanations of the behavior of people and who wrote in the preface to *Miss Julia:* "What we want to see are . . . the wires, the machinery. We want to investigate the box with the false bottom, touch the magic ring in order to find the future, and look into the cards to discover how they are marked."

An important character should be enriched and elaborated not alone to make that person interesting, but in order to illuminate other characters and to advance the action. Miss Gallaway has put her finger on an excellent example of this in Werfel's *Jacobowsky and the Colonel:*

Jacobowsky has an unusually rich character. He is described as "a heavy-set man of middle age with a rosy round face and fine eyes with long lashes. He is dressed in scrupulous neatness in a somewhat old-fashioned . . . cutaway. His manner . . . is courteous. . . . His speech is well considered, stylistically perfect, sometimes to the point of formalism. . . . Only occasionally a trace of nervousness . . . makes it apparent that his self-discipline is the result of his battle with fate." This is for the reader. The audience learns more about him. Evidently he is *sociable,* because he goes out in an air raid to bring *marrons glacés* to help the ladies pass the trying night, and because he selects in the shelter a place next to an old lady and promptly begins to chat with her, telling her some of his past life. He has a *fatalistic* attitude toward life; on his first entrance during the air raid someone teases him for thinking himself indestructible, and he replies with a mathematical calculation on his chances of getting hit. He is both fatalistic and *sentimental* when, forced to flee, he has to leave behind not only his valuable antique furniture, but also his cherished Persian rugs that are to him a symbol of home. Again he reveals his fatalism when Stjerbinsky challenges him to a duel and he accepts, asking Stjerbinsky first to show him how the pistol works. He is *shrewd finan-*

cially in his purchase of the automobile, and later when Stjerbinsky taunts him with securing his money belt as a last precaution before going to sleep. He is *impractical* in mechanical and physical ways, not being able to shoot, swim, nor drive a car. Yet he is highly *resourceful* in providing food and gasoline for the escape, and endearingly *attentive to the needs of others,* providing cognac for the Colonel and even chocolates for Marianne's little dog. He yells with *fright* and *rage* when his car will not go, and sweats with *nervousness* when the Germans question him. He shows his *pride* when he does not take offense at Stjerbinsky's arrogance, and when he refuses to shake hands with Stjerbinsky. He reveals *patience* as Stjerbinsky again and again forgets his name, as they start their desperate flight by going first into the jaws of the Germans to get the Colonel's sweetheart, as he addresses the dead Kamnitzer in the *Père Clairon,* "You were impatient." He is *hot-tempered, gallant, tactful, optimistic, happy,* and deeply *humorous,* to end the list of his qualities without further elaborating the incidents which plant them. Naturally these incidents are not used solely to characterize Jacobowsky; they characterize also the persons with whom he has the scenes; and many, if not most, of the incidents advance the action.

Details That Count

It is hardly necessary to say not only that the labor of characterization is great, but that it also entails the exercise of an enormous amount of care and judgment. You must know when you are using just enough detail and when you may be using too much. "Your principal characters have had a childhood," says Raphaelson, "things that formed them, moving events in their lives. Go over your play and see if John's childhood emerges anywhere." Yet you must select only those events that are needed, those that will be really functional.

Lady Gregory, who helped to found the Abbey Theatre in Dublin and who wrote so many characterful folk-comedies, was unusually conscious of both the peaks of success and the pitfalls of failure involved in the creation of characters. In a lecture that she gave in Boston forty years ago she asked such questions as these: Can you tell your story with fewer characters? Can you put your characters in closer personal touch with one another? Are they ordinary people in extraordinary circumstances, or extraordinary people in ordinary circumstances? However real your characters may be, Lady Gregory observed, you must "lift them off the ground a bit. Passion does it in tragedy; exaggeration, in comedy."

Sometimes it is a very small thing that shows the care of the fine dramatist and pays off enormously in characterization and in effect on an audience. A case in point is the change of two words between the first draft of *A Doll's House* and the final version. As Ibsen originally wrote that scene in the last act where Torvald reads the note from Krogstad in which he says he has repented and will not press the charge of forgery against her, Torvald cried: "Nora! We are saved!" By the little change of "we are saved" to "I am saved!" Ibsen drove home the selfish egotism of Torvald and completely prepared the ground for Nora's "Sit down, Torvald. You and I have much to say to one another . . . For eight years I have been living here with a strange man."

Must Characters "Grow"?

There are many strange and foolish dogmas about important characters. One is that they must change and develop. Archer questions this. He points out that character is "a complex of intellectual, emotional, and nervous habits," that "some of these are innate and temperamental," and he asks whether it is possible for a character to alter, within the limits of a play, "the mental habits underlying his speech and actions . . . Is it consistent with the usual and desirable time-limits of drama? In the long process of a novel, there may be time for the gradual alteration of habits; in the drama, which normally consists of a single crisis [the climax of the play], any real change of character would have to be of a catastrophic nature. . . . By development of character, I think they mean, not change, but rather unveiling, disclosure. The word 'development' might be very aptly used in the photographic sense. A drama ought to bring out character as the photographer's chemicals 'bring out' the forms latent in the negative.

But this is quite a different thing from development in the sense of growth or radical change. In all modern drama, there is perhaps no character who 'develops,' in the ordinary sense of the word, so startlingly as Ibsen's Nora; and we cannot but feel that the poet has compressed into a week an evolution which, in fact, would have demanded many months."

Now, whether or not Archer is right in his criticism of Nora's change, Egri quotes the first half of Archer's last sentence in which he records this development, and then writes: "Look at any truly great play and you will see the same point illustrated." Using the name of the play, but presumably meaning the character of the title role—since that is the context, and since this section of his book is called "Character Growth"—he says: "*Othello* starts with love, ends with jealousy, murder, and suicide. . . . *Hedda Gabler* starts with egotism, ends with suicide. . . . *Hamlet* starts with suspicion, ends with murder." I should say that, at least with Hedda and Hamlet, Egri is mistaking a change of action for a change of character. Hedda and Hamlet are the same people at the end as they are in the beginning, except that they have suffered and died.

The rule that characters must develop *as characters* is as much honored in the breach as many of the other rules that critics have tried to impose on playwriting. Is there any major character development in *The Cherry Orchard, Oedipus Rex, Hamlet, Street Scene, The Death of a Salesman, The Miser, A Streetcar*

Named Desire, The Little Foxes, Juno and the Paycock, The Merchant of Venice, Liliom, Justice, The Lower Depths, Mr. Roberts, Cyrano de Bergerac, Riders to the Sea, The Weavers, The Father, Miss Julia, or *Candida?* If there is, that is not the dominant factor. Development of character is a potent and important tool in some great plays as well as some merely successful ones, but it is not essential.

Doctrinaire statements about character are as dangerous as doctrinaire statements about almost anything else in playwriting. Believe only that characterization is of as much importance as plot. Plot can never make characters; the writer must find or create the people that animate a story. But characters can and do make plot. Egri sums this up acutely when he writes: "There must be something to *generate* tension, something to *create* complication, without any conscious [?] attempt on the playwright's part to do so. There must be a force which will unify all parts, a force out of which they will grow as naturally as limbs grow from the body. We think we know what that force is: human character."

5

Wills in Conflict

What we ask of the theatre is defined by the action of a *will* striving toward a goal, and conscious of the means which it employs . . . the dramatic species is defined by the nature of the obstacles encountered by this will.

BRUNETIÈRE

Where There's a Will There's a Play

CONFLICT HAS SEEMED TO MANY PLAYWRIGHTS AND critics to be the soul of drama. They feel that, though it may play a part in other forms of literature, conflict is the distinguishing mark of drama.

These theorists almost always look to a single source for conflict. This is a battle of wills. It is usually a battle between the wills of two principals in a play; it is sometimes a struggle of one man against circumstance. They like to call one of the two chief characters the protagonist and the other the antagonist—a learned way of saying hero and villain. They see a man with a will, or desire, confronted by an obstacle. If the obstacle is not another man, it may be fate, a group of men, a condition of life, a vital and powerful idea.

These theorizings seem to me to present difficulties. There are great plays without a battle of wills and without major conflicts. There are effective plays with no protagonist, with more than one hero, with no villain, or with no single obstacle.

Exceptions to the Rule

It was in 1863 that Gustav Freytag, the German playwright and critic, wrote in *The Technique of the Drama:* "The drama must have only one chief hero, about whom all persons . . . arrange themselves." This was true enough until the birth of the realistic drama twenty years later. Emphasis on the rights of the individual and also on the rights of the social group—so dominant in late nineteenth-century thought—drew the playwright away from the lone hero. The dramatist gave three or more people equal place in his plot, or he made whole groups his hero. Where is the lone protagonist of conscious will in *Ghosts, The Wild Duck, Rosmersholm, Design for Living, The Cherry Orchard, Our Town, The Lower Depths, Grand Hotel, The Women, Desire Under the Elms, The Weavers, The Plow and the Stars, Outward Bound, The Glass Menagerie, Street Scene, Awake and Sing, The Great God Brown, Liliom, Dead End, What Price Glory?*, or *Journey's End?* The hero becomes multiple in *The Weavers, Bury the Dead,* and *Man and the Masses. Liliom* and *Journey's End* have two chief and equal figures, and they have no villains. *Elizabeth the Queen* has characters in conflict; but Elizabeth and Essex are both protagonists and both antagonists, while Cecil and Bacon play rudimentary villains.

The protagonist, we are told, must be made sympathetic by his attractiveness, his ideals and aims, his moral or spiritual beauty, his daring, devotion, or self-sacrifice. And there are plenty of heroes and heroines who meet this test. But there are also people like Hedda Gabler, Falder in *Justice,* the Negro in *The Emperor Jones,* McLeod in *Detective Story,* who are neither heroes nor villains and yet are the central figures of their plays.

Another dictum about heroes is that they must be dynamic. They usually are. But what about poor Othello, who has to be lured and cozened into action, and then the action is evil and destructive? What is dynamic in Falder or Hedda or Harry Van and Irene in *Idiot's Delight?* There is no dynamic hero in *The Iceman Cometh* or *Tobacco Road* or most of Chekhov's plays.

Even so general a rule as that the hero's objective must be simple and clearly revealed finds an exception in *Liliom.* The objective is as twofold as the protagonists and it becomes completely clear only in the last line.

The "Pivotal Character"

Bemused with Greek and Latin words and pseudo-Greek theories, some of our analysts of drama go on to play tricks with another bit of verbiage—the "pivotal character." "Without a pivotal character," says Egri, "there is no play. The pivotal character is the one who creates conflict and makes the play move forward. The pivotal character knows what he wants. Without him the play flounders . . . in fact there is no play." Just above this statement, Egri writes: "The pivotal character is the *protagonist.*" But further on, he discloses that Iago is the pivotal character in *Othello,* Krogstad in *A Doll's House,* the parents in *Romeo and Juliet.* Are these protagonists?

"Villain" Gives Way to "Obstacle"

Protagonist versus antagonist, hero against villain, is not so simple a matter as it ought to be. *Elizabeth the Queen* is too complex for the formula. *Romeo and Juliet* doesn't really fit it. In *Richard III,* the will is the will of the villain, and a laggard hero becomes a rather tardy obstacle. Today we do not believe, with Freytag, that "the opposing power must be made visible in a human presentation." The opposing power may be quite invisible, as in *Justice, Street Scene, The Lower Depths, Outward Bound, The Silver Box, Young Woodley, Dead End, Damaged Goods, The Death of a*

Salesman, and *The Winslow Boy.* More likely it resides in the actions of a man or a woman whose nature is no more evil than that of the hero. We are wary of villainous antagonists.

Sometimes "objective" and "obstacle" replace or amplify "protagonist" and "antagonist"; they personify the "wills" of hero and villain.

The "obstacle" is a term that has been used to mean either the villain, some rather remote product of his activity, the ambitions or desires of another type of man, the behavior of some perfectly normal people like the Montagues and the Capulets, or some idea or fact, some social convention or prejudice. "The obstacle should be equal to the hero's will. An overwhelming obstacle is dangerous," says one writer; yet the Greeks did pretty well with fate and the laws of the gods. This matter of obstacle against objective may sometimes sound quite complex: "Occasionally the obstacle is a mutually exclusive double objective." Which means that, in *Elizabeth the Queen,* Elizabeth wants to keep both her throne and her lover, while Essex wants to take over the power through love and yet feels that, under the conditions of the play, he would not make the kind of king he thinks he ought to be.

Today the obstacle has broadened out from a villain and his destructive desires to social villainies—the law's destructive force in *Justice,* the environment of poverty in *Dead End* and *Street Scene.* It has dipped into things out of the past—the sexual sins of the father in *Ghosts,* an old forgery in *A Doll's House,* ingrained incompetence in *The Cherry Orchard,* sterility in *Tomorrow and Tomorrow.*

Whether there is an obstacle in human form or human actions, or an obstacle made up of social forces or past events, the beginning playwright must grasp the obvious and very important fact that once the obstacle is surmounted or proved insurmountable, the play is over. If the obstacle is in danger of disappearing too early in the evening, the job of the playwright is to anticipate this by subtly introducing a new obstacle *before* the other is out of the way. He cannot do it afterwards.

The Paradox of Tragedy

Offhand it would seem that a hero's success or failure in attaining his objective and overcoming the final obstacle makes a play a comedy or a tragedy. Usually it does, but not always. There are a number of very great tragedies in which the hero achieves his objective. Hamlet takes the King's life, though he loses his own. Oedipus desires something higher than his own life, of greater value than his throne or his eyesight—the good of the state—and this he secures. Romeo and Juliet, united in death, are nearer their objective than they could have been if she had had to marry Paris, or he had been executed for killing Tybalt while she lived on. The secret of successful tragedy—and I am using "successful" in both its higher and its baser sense—is to leave the audience with the feeling that the death of the hero accomplished something. This is the tragedy of fulfilment, not the tragedy of frustration. It produces what Aristotle called "catharsis." This purging of emotion through tragedy can come only where there is either a certain spiritual greatness in the hero and/or a sense of the salutary in the outcome. It is the explanation of why, as Rowe puts it, "a great tragedy is one of the supreme paradoxes of experience. The audience is confronted with the full sweep and absoluteness of evil and suffering, and the effect at the resolution is a mood at once of exaltation and serenity."

Conflicts Over Conflict

The difficulty with most of the theories recounted in this chapter is the difficulty with many theories on other things. They are true in many cases; they may be true in most cases; but they are not true in *all* cases. Brunetière was blind to this when he wrote: "The theatre in general is nothing but the place for the development of the human will, attacking the obstacles opposed to it by destiny, fortune, or circumstance."

Certain critics stress the human will as the essence of drama because opposed wills make conflict, create dramatic struggle, and they believe that all drama is built out of such conflict. The trouble with this all-inclusive theory is twofold. First, there are many fine plays without conflict of wills. Second, there are many fine plays in which there is no all-over conflict, dramas in which the conflict is confined only to scenes or sequences of scenes.

I think Raphaelson is ignoring these two facts when he says: "A play deals with conflict. I have never written one that didn't have conflict and I don't know of any I have seen without conflict—people against each other, a man against himself, a man against society, a man against the gods—it is all conflict." Raphaelson has failed to note that in many a play the struggle is not between human wills, and that, while he will find some sort of conflict in all plays, it may lie only in individual scenes and may not be the dominating, over-all pattern. "A stand-up fight between will and will," said Archer, ". . . is no doubt one of the intensest forms of drama. But it is comparatively rare, at any rate as the formula of a whole play. In individual scenes a conflict of will is frequent enough; but it is, after all, only one among a multitude of equally telling forms of drama."

Archer cites a number of plays to prove his point. "Where, for instance, is the struggle in the *Agamemnon?*" Oedipus "does not struggle at all. . . . In the actual course of the tragedy he simply writhes under one revelation after another of bygone error and unwitting crime. It would be a mere play upon words to recognize as dramatic 'struggle' the writhing of a worm on a hook." As for Othello, "There is no struggle, no conflict, between him and Iago. It is Iago alone who exerts any will; neither Othello nor Desdemona makes the smallest fight." "Where is the conflict in *As You Like It*?" "Or take . . . Ibsen's *Ghosts*—in what valid sense can it be said that tragedy shows us will struggling against obstacles?"

Alan Thompson does not go quite so far as Archer. He concedes that "conflict is ordinarily the chief source of dramatic interest," but, he says, "it is no absolute necessity." He suggests *The Trojan Women* and *Riders to the Sea* as great plays without an over-all pattern of conflict. Lawson cites *The Great God Brown* as "a play in which *the conscious will plays no part at all.*" As examples of plays in which conflict of wills is not the dominant note I might mention *Ah, Wilderness!*, *Grand Hotel*, *Dinner at Eight*, *Our Town*, *The Insect Comedy*, *The Lady in the Dark*, *The Skin of Our Teeth*, and *The Magnificent Yankee*.

Thompson has a sage explanation for the decline of the hero, the man of powerful will, as the basis for modern drama. "The old pieties that fostered heroism have largely passed away, along with the old monarchies and aristocracies. . . . The older opportunities for glory through personal achievement have dwindled everywhere with the increase in economic and social interdependence, with the increase in the complexity of social organization. The sciences also have had a large share in destroying the heroic tradition by seeming to demonstrate how petty, bestial, and physically conditioned are all men. A philosophy of flux, a belief that no standards are absolute and that all things change with the shifting forces of a blind and indifferent Nature, has come to dominate the thoughts of modern man." That is why "in recent times we have come increasingly to concern ourselves with the ordinary mortal who is acted upon more than acting, and less and less with the exceptional hero who wills and fights on the grand scale." "Chekhov's plays," Thompson points out, "are populated by characters whose absence of strong will, or inability to exert it, is the very source of the playwright's tragicomic effects." If he had written *The Anatomy of Drama* in 1950 instead of 1946, he might have mentioned *The Death of a Salesman* as a brilliant study of the atrophy of the will in an ordinary mortal.

Protagonist and antagonist, hero and villain, objective and obstacle, the conflict of wills, conflict itself as an over-all pattern—all these are merely tools that are useful in the craft of playwriting. They are not the Mosaic tables of dramaturgy. They form no general and immutable law. But, quite as clearly, they are still potent, and their elements should be used when they suit the material of the playwright.

6

The Essential Unity

I would we were all of one mind and one mind good.

SHAKESPEARE

Only One Unity for the Greeks—Action

ARISTOTLE WAS NOT TO BLAME. FIRST CRITIC OF THE drama and first teacher of playwriting, he was responsible for only one of the three unities–the unities of time, of place, and of action–which cursed the European theatre from the Renaissance until 1700.

Aristotle never saw the great Greek tragedies of Aeschylus, Sophocles, and Euripides. He read them in manuscript after the last of these writers had been dead a hundred years. What he tried to do was to set down his observations on a very special kind of religious and stylized drama and to analyze the secrets of their peculiar kind of power.

In doing this, he stressed what has been called unity of action, though it might better be called unity of story or, indeed, unity of the whole play. "The structural unity of the parts," he wrote, "is such that, if any one of them is displaced or removed, the whole will be disjointed and disturbed. For a thing whose presence or absence makes no visible difference is not an organic part of the whole." He said nothing about unity of place, and the only thing he wrote about the element of time was that "tragedy endeavors, as far as possible, to confine itself to a single revolution of the sun or but slightly to exceed this limit." He stated this as a fact in Greek tragedy; he did not argue its merit. The only unity that he urged as essential was the unity of action.

Unity of Time and Place a Renaissance Invention

It was almost nineteen hundred years later that a man of the Renaissance, Lodovico Castelvetro, invented the additional unities of time and place: "The time of the representation and that of the action presented must be exactly coincidental . . . and the scene of the action must be constant." These words appeared in 1570, and, with the aid of people who seem not to have read Aristotle's *Poetics*, either in the Greek edition of 1498 or the Italian version of 1549, Castelvetro succeeded in attributing to the great Greek the authorship of the three "Aristotelian" unities.

These unities dominated tragedy for more than a century and a half, though great and popular dramatists like Shakespeare and Lope de Vega paid no attention to them. In the eighteenth century Goldoni wrote: "If Aristotle were now alive, he would cancel the obnoxious rule, for a thousand absurdities, a thousand blunders and improprieties are caused by it. . . . Those haters of novelty who insist on a complete accord with bygone standards appear to be like physicians who refuse to prescribe quinine for the sole reason that Hippocrates or Galen had not yet adopted it."

Some "Non-Stop" Experiments in Playwriting

The unities of time and place have, indeed, been observed by a few modern playwrights. Strindberg became enamored of the idea in the late '80's and wrote in connection with *Miss Julia:* "I have tried to abolish the division into acts. And I have done this because I have come to fear that our decreasing capacity for illusion might be unfavorably affected by intermissions during which the spectator would have time to reflect and to get away from the suggestive influence of the author-hypnotist. . . . My hope is for a public educated to the point where it can sit through a whole-evening performance in a single act." He got no further, however, than the hour and a quarter of *Miss Julia* with a sort of ballet in the middle. Charles Rann Kennedy wrote *The Servant in the House,* Bernard Shaw *Getting Married,* and Somerset Maugham *The Bread Winner* in continuous action, but divided the plays into normal acts by the dropping and raising of the curtain in the course of the play.

George M. Cohan's *Pigeons and People* and Philip Barry's *Hotel Universe* were played without act divisions, but the strain on the attention of the audience helped to make them failures.

One Unity Is Essential

Unity of action is another matter. Action meant to Aristotle the dramatic story. We can translate it as the play itself. And certainly unity of some sort is absolutely essential to any effective production, whether tragedy, drama, or comedy.

In another connection, perhaps, Rowe has put his finger on three processes that make for unity: "Elimination of the unessential, arrangement by which to compress as much significant action as possible into each continuous scene, and suggestion by what is said and done on the stage of a great deal that has happened off-stage," the whole process working "toward unity, proportion, economy, and intensity."

One of the essentials of unity—and one of its virtues—is economy of means. Though you may have to tell your audience an important thing three times, you must never annoy or distract playgoers with useless material, unimportant detail. You should make one scene or even one speech do two things at the same time, if both can be made clear and effective. Don't give over a whole scene merely to showing that your hero is hot tempered while the plot stands still. You should show he is hot tempered in a scene that advances the story or introduces a complication. Boil your plot down to its essentials and expand on those. Use no more elements of action, no more dramatic episodes, than you need in order to develop convincingly the plot, characters, and theme, if you have a theme. Selection and condensation are as hard a part of the work of play construction as developing plot and characters to begin with. Voltaire said: "Ask anyone who has crowded too many events into his play what the reason for this fault is; if he is honest he will tell you that he lacked the inventive genius to fill his play with a single action."

If a play has unity, it is not cluttered with scenes unrelated to the story that it tells and to the characters it needs to tell the story. There should be a minimum of discursive or intrusive material, and this minimum can be permitted only because it entertains without distracting. The play *might* be better without it; so make sure that such material does not bewilder or distract. Above all, there must be no scenes or even speeches that may arouse false expectations or lead an audience astray.

Unity of Mood

There are many examples of successful and respectable plays in which unity of action in the narrowest sense does not seem to be the outstanding feature, yet in which, beneath the surface of a shallow or wandering plot, a real unity actually exists. An example is *Life with Father.* Plotwise, it is frightfully meager: Mother wants to get Father baptized, and in the end she succeeds. Along the way there are innumerable amusing scenes and flavorous incidents that have nothing to do with her reverent end. But the play has, nevertheless, complete unity of mood—the mood of picturesque and hilarious family life in the 1880's—and there are no laggard or distracting scenes.

Unity of mood is essential. This does not mean that there can be no laughter in a serious drama or even in a tragedy. It does mean that one mood is clearly dominant. Philip Barry's brilliant and fantastic *White Wings* was a failure, as Krows points out, because of a confusion, even a discord, of tones: "Sometimes it was comedy, sometimes farce, and sometimes tragedy—none of which needed to be wholly excluded, but all save one of which should have been subordinated to a controlling spirit."

Unity of Many Kinds

Read any number of good, effective, successful plays, long or short, and you will find that almost all possess an inner unity—usually of plot development, sometimes of mood, sometimes of character relationships. Unity is absolutely essential in a one-act play; everything in Barrie's *The Twelve Pound Look* is built around the reaction of a desperately courageous woman to her pompous and deadly ex-husband; everything in Synge's *Riders to the Sea* leads to the mother's reaction to the final tragedy. In *Oedipus Rex* and *Arsenic and Old Lace* you find in almost equal measure unity of both action and mood. *The Little Foxes* is just as tight and unified as any of Ibsen's best plays. Rostand was not exactly economical of means in *Cyrano de Bergerac,* but the characters and speeches that may be technically superfluous to the story are all brilliant ornaments to a character and a period that excuse—indeed, demand—such ornaments. The actual plot of Elmer Rice's *Street Scene*—the action built around the infidelity of Maurrant's wife—occupies, as Miss Gallaway points out, less than a quarter of the play, but the other events and the other characters—the social atmosphere of a mean street—form a solid and unifying matrix that seems to shape the action within it. The movement of O'Casey's *The Plow and the Stars* is as poorly plotted, as random a series of events, as the Easter Rebellion that is its background, but the play is unified by the superb handling of mood and character. The same thing can be said for the virtues of Gorki's *The Lower Depths,* but the small plot he provides is more compact. Chekhov's *The Cherry Orchard,* like most of his plays, has unity of mood. It is hard to find much unity of action in O'Neill's *Ah, Wilderness!* or in Hecht and MacArthur's *The Front Page,* but each is held together and made entertaining by its concentration on a slice of American life. Though Sherriff's *Journey's End* has three plots from which dramatic action flows—the relations of Raleigh and Stanhope, the cowardice of Hippert, and events of the war on one sector of the front—the play is unified by the tense interrelation of its three forms of action.

The Use of Subplot

Castelvetro, who provided the unities that Aristotle missed, laid down the rule: "No drama can be praiseworthy which has not two actions, that is, two plots, though one is principal and the other accessory." Although Shakespeare used the subplot freely in most of his comedies, he eschewed it in his tragedies, and with the coming of realism the subsidiary plot fell into disfavor. It had been at its best only when its solution came at the same time as the solution of the main plot, and played a part in that solution. There are traces of subplots in some of Ibsen's plays, but they are no more than vestiges, and their climaxes operate generally off-stage. In *A Doll's House* the love story of Mrs. Linde and Krogstad, culminating in the last act, would have saved Nora from exposure as a forger if Ibsen had wanted to write a conventionally happy ending. Molnar runs a subplot clear through *Liliom*—the love story of the heroine's girl-friend Marie and Wolf, Marie's comic lover and successful husband. It has no effect on the main plot, but it adds to the reality of the play and serves as a kind of ironic contrast to the tortuous and tortured love story of Julie and Liliom. Today the subplot is still a stand-by in musical shows; taking over a portion of the all-too-short time left for the main plot, it provides for the humor of comedian and soubrette.

The Danger in the Thesis Play

Achieving unity is a very real problem for the man who wants to write a thesis play, a play of propaganda. Theme and characters are very difficult to unite. Ibsen united them consummately in *A Doll's House* and *Ghosts;* Galsworthy succeeded almost as well in *Justice* and *Loyalties.* But the task is usually beyond the reach of the apprentice playwright because, as Alan Thompson has put it in *The Anatomy of Drama,* "forcing his characters to fit a thesis renders them unreal, but subordinating his thesis to lifelike characterization renders it confused or insignificant."

Fewer Acts—More Sets?

Are there any mechanical aids to the effect of unity, aids that are easy and almost as potent as continuous action, which I have already discussed? Down through the centuries and notably in the past few years there has been a tendency to cut down the number of acts and, particularly, the number of intermissions. In itself this will not produce *actual* unity, though it may create an effect of *apparent* unity and give a sense of more solid construction.

From the time of Horace, just before the birth of Christ, until the last quarter of the nineteenth century the great bulk of plays were written (or printed) in five acts. This was because the Roman, in his *Ars Poetica,* had said they ought to be so written. Aristotle had set up five divisions in the action's progress—exposition, complication, climax, denouement, and catastrophe—but he had never described them as separate acts. Noting that there were four choral passages in Greek tragedies, with acted scenes before, in between, and after, Horace set up the five-act play form and the playwrights of most of Europe accepted it. Lope de Vega, writing in the time of Shakespeare, ignored the rule, wrote in three acts, and set the fashion for Calderon and many another Spanish playwright. I am sure Shakespeare, also, ignored Horace, for, though editions of his plays after his death divided them into five acts, the twenty plays that were pirated and published in quartos during his lifetime had no act divisions.

The nineteenth-century realists, striving for more compact and powerful effects and realizing, as Strindberg pointed out, that intermissions let down the tension in the audience that the previous act had built up, reduced the number of acts to four and then to three. Today plays with four or more scenes are seldom given with more than two intermissions. Perhaps because the motion picture has accustomed our audiences to an hour and half or two hours of continuous entertainment, the tendency toward a single pause during the evening, which began with *Liliom,* has rapidly established itself through plays like *Dream Girl, I Remember Mama, The Glass Menagerie, The Madwoman of Chaillot, Mr. Roberts, The Death of a Salesman, The Cocktail Party,* and *The Country Girl.*

Of course cutting down on intermissions doesn't necessarily mean reducing the number of scenes. *Liliom* had seven scenes in addition to a prologue in pantomime. Though we look at the same physical set through the two acts of *The Death of a Salesman,* we see at least eighteen separate scenes of both the past and the present.

Obviously the playwright should use as many different settings as seem necessary to tell his story with the greatest effectiveness. Shakespeare used as many as forty-two in *Antony and Cleopatra.* Ibsen himself had thirty-five sets in *Peer Gynt.* I could give you a long list of New York successes, from *Romance, Liliom, The Emperor Jones,* and *The Hairy Ape* through *The Lady in the Dark* to *Anne of the Hundred Days* and *The Country Girl* that have used a considerable number of different sets.

Experiments in physical production are always worthwhile—when you are ready for them. In *Desire Under the Elms* O'Neill combined in one setting the exterior and four rooms of a farmhouse, and in *The Voice of the Turtle* Van Druten showed three rooms of an apartment at the same time. The multiple set worked equally well in *Come Back, Little Sheba, The Member of the Wedding,* and *The Rose Tattoo. The Glass Menagerie* and *A Streetcar Named Desire* combined interiors and exteriors by using the painted gauze of long ago. In *The Death of a Salesman* one setting served for the modern reality of three rooms in a house, two offices, and a restaurant of today and various locales of the past. Elmer Rice in his first play, *On Trial,* elected to tell his story in reverse, beginning with a scene in court and going backward thirteen years to present the evidence that was to clear the heroine of murder. Twenty years later George S. Kaufman and Moss Hart applied the same technique to *Merrily We Roll Along.* Two old plays, *Paid in Full* and *Under Cover,* each had an act that overlapped the last few minutes of the preceding act. A graduate student of mine tried the experiment of beginning his play with act two and going back to act one—which held a necessary clue to the nature and behavior of his characters—only at the end of the play.

Curtain Lines

Though realism reduced the number of acts and lessened the need for "strong curtain lines" to hold the interest of audiences through intermissions, many playwrights still strove to place the last ounce of shock or suspense in the final line of an act. Recall, for instance, the end of the first act of *Ghosts.* Twenty years before, Mrs. Alving had heard her husband making love to a servant in the conservatory. Now as she stands in the neighboring room with Pastor Manders, she hears the servant Regina—her husband's daughter by that old affair—say to her son, "Oswald! Are you mad? Let me go!" As Mrs. Alving reacts in horror, the Pastor asks, "What can be the matter? What is it, Mrs. Alving?" She replies, "Ghosts! The couple from the conservatory—risen again!" Most serious playwrights, however, avoided such strong curtain lines. Rejecting what they felt was theatrical effect, they preferred to ease off after a dramatic climax and to bring down the curtain on quieter dialogue or action. In your own curtain lines, you have the choice between the strong, or theatrical, and the restrained, or "natural." The nature of your play will probably determine this for you.

If you go for a strong curtain, be careful that it is not *too* strong. Thompson cites the final curtain of Gerhardt Hauptmann's *Before Sunrise:* "The heroine commits suicide with a hunting knife, off-stage are heard the yells of her drunken father, and the curtain falls upon the continuous screaming of the maid. Such a heaping up of horrors justifies incredulous laughter." One of my students had a similar difficulty in an early draft of the end of his first act. Toward the beginning of the scene, we had learned that a character who might be described as the villain of the piece was having an affair with the wife of a manufacturer in whose home he was visiting. The writer brought down his first curtain with the discovery that the man had seduced a young girl who was also staying in the house, and with the almost instantaneous explosion of the manufacturer's powder plant.

The One-set Show

The high cost of production on Broadway is leading new playwrights to follow too sedulously the fashion that Ibsen established—and sometimes ignored—for the "one-set show." Since *A Doll's House* there have been a long string of successful plays with only one setting—*The Playboy of the Western World, Heartbreak House, Street Scene, Candida, Dead End, Idiot's Delight, The Petrified Forest, Awake and Sing, Tobacco Road, The Hasty Heart, The Little Foxes, Born Yesterday, The Lady's Not for Burning, Detective Story,* to name only a few. With no bow to commercialism, I think it is wise for the beginning playwright to set himself the problem of writing the conventional three-act play laid in one or at most two settings. Unity of place may aid him in achieving unity of action. But, as he develops his talent, he should not hesitate to use a plot that requires many backgrounds.

Ibsen's Way to Unity of Action

The one-set show cannot be an infallible key to unity, but the way that Ibsen began his drama in such a set can be a definite help in uniting characters and story in a tight, unified plot. This is the device, which the Greeks also used, of starting the action of a play as close as possible to its turning point, instead of going back, as Shakespeare often did, to the moments in the past when the seeds were sown that later grew into conflict and climax. The novelist tells the whole story, often in flashbacks. The playwright is required by the theatre to select only the most important material, the material that leads as quickly as possible to the major dramatic crisis. Through exposition he supplies the needed background. With *A Doll's House,* Ibsen found the secret of starting a play well toward the end of the story, and of using exposition at the beginning to create suspense and using it again and again throughout the evening to drive the characters on through conflict after conflict to the final climax of the drama. Krows says: "Great plays usually have the appearance, at least, of beginning *in media res.* The audience comes to see the struggle, not the training of the fighters." In discussing *Oedipus Rex* on that exceptional radio program *Invitation to Learning,* Lyman Bryson noted that "the play starts when all this past action begins to bear fruit in trouble," and Louis Kronenberger commented: "Oh, almost all great plays start when most of the action is behind one." In Shakespeare's finest play, *Hamlet,* he started nearer the climax of his story than he usually did and nearer than any notable dramatist from his day to Ibsen's.

7

The Nature of Dramatic Action

Action in drama causes more confusion in the minds of apprentice authors than, perhaps, any other part of it.

ST. JOHN ERVINE

Action Is Speech More Than Movement

IT WOULD HAVE BEEN A VERY GOOD THING INDEED IF THE translators of Aristotle had never used the English word "action" or its equivalent in other languages for the Greek word πράξις. Occasionally they replaced it by "fable"; but if they had used "plot" or "plot development," we should be a lot better off today. Then no student who comes upon Aristotle's thoughts on tragedy would make the mistake of believing that action means physical movement.

Unfortunately, as Alan Thompson observes, the word "action" is ambiguous. "In ordinary usage it means bodily action—all muscular movements except those of speech. In this sense, moving our hands and legs is 'action' but wagging our tongues is not. This distinction is often justified in life, as when we wish that a person would 'talk less and do more'; but when applied to the drama it leads to a grave misapprehension, for it causes people to overlook the fact that *the principal form of dramatic action is speech.*"

St. John Ervine gets a good deal of fun out of making the same point by *reductio ad absurdum:* "There are people who fondly imagine that when we speak of action in a play, we mean that a character rises from one seat and sits upon another. They think there is movement in a play when people enter or go out. When you speak of action to them, they immediately imagine that you mean *doing things.* Thus when a character sits on his hat or falls over a rug, they say to themselves, 'That is action. This is movement!' "

Having spiked the notion that action is bustle or mere physical movement, Ervine goes on to say what it is: "Action is of several sorts. It may consist of what people do; it may consist of what they say; it may consist of what they think . . . the activity lies in their power to carry the play forward from one state to another."

Another playwright, Langdon Mitchell, once pointed out that the "staged" collision of two steam engines at a state fair may be exciting to watch, but it is not dramatic, as we use the word in the theatre. "Nothing is dramatic that is not human and psychological." Action may be either violent or quiet and yet be equally powerful. In demonstration he cited the killing of Caesar and the kiss of Judas.

Except for minor pieces of business and minor conversations—and the fewer of these, the better—the action of a scene or act is usually continuous. By means of words, pantomime, and movement it presents the plot of the play in terms of the theatre. It is the embodiment of the plot as set down in the playscript, just as the plot is the embodiment of the story as extracted, organized, and condensed to form the scenario of the play.

Sometimes, though very rarely, the action essential to a drama may not be continuous, and may occupy only a part of the playing time. This happens in *Street Scene*, but the remainder of the drama, while not action in the technical sense, surrounds the plot with the atmosphere it needs to make it effective. There is even less action in *The Cherry Orchard*. It is rare, however, that true action plays so small a part in an effective play.

Violent Action Better Off-stage

Physical action is rarely as important as what might be called spiritual action, the action of characters as conveyed by words, and it is a lot more troublesome. The playwright has to decide what kinds of physical action in his story are proper on the stage, and what kinds are better played off-stage. This is particularly important when the action is violent. A slap, a physical fight, a murder may rightly be shown in front of the audience, but too many such bits of "action" will spoil the effect of the play, bring it down to melodrama, even make it ludicrous.

There was considerable justification for the Greek rule that violence should not be shown on-stage. Some violence is far better done off-stage because it can thus stimulate the emotions more strongly through the audience's imagination. The blinding of Oedipus is such a piece of violence. When Shakespeare called for the blinding on-stage of Gloucester in *King Lear,* he risked driving horror over into nausea or bringing the audience up sharply to the realization that it is all a clever—or a bungling—pretence. No one, I think, has ever tried to burn Joan of Arc on a stage fire.

It is always wise to avoid technical displays such as a forest fire or a stormy sea. They cannot "come off," and, if they could, the miracle of their accomplishment would distract the audience from the words or the emotions of the characters. A fire or a storm can be more effectively conveyed through a window and by the comments of the people on-stage.

A murder can be made much more effective if the characters begin the scene of violence on-stage, and in their struggles retreat through a door for the kill. In connection with *Street Scene,* Miss Gallaway demonstrates the effectiveness of violence played partly on-stage and partly off. "Maurrant goes upstairs [from the street into an unseen room in the apartment house] to kill his wife. There is a scream and a shot. Then Sankey [the lover] appears at the window screaming for help. Maurrant drags him away and there is another shot. Later, Mrs. Maurrant is carried downstairs on a stretcher, to die as Rose tries to talk to her." The drowning of the crippled child in *Little Eyolf* is most effectively conveyed when the parents in their room hear a voice off-stage crying: "The crutch is floating."

Physical action that goes beyond walking about on the stage has only a small part in most good drama, and physical violence a still smaller part. Out of about sixty plays that have run for more than 499 performances on Broadway, you have to stretch the definition of physical action pretty far to get fifteen in which it appears. In the Burns Mantle lists of the ten best plays of each season, the proportion is a little smaller. There is no discoverable pattern based on the nature of the particular play. *What Price Glory?* has a good deal of physical action; another war play, *Journey's End,* has almost none. *Liliom,* despite its very "physical" hero, has only one slap and the hold-up and suicide scene. Galsworthy's *Escape* has a great deal of physical movement, though no real violence, while another of his thesis plays, *The Silver Box,* has neither. *A Streetcar Named Desire,* though its values depend on character, has a fight and a rape. Gorki's *The Lower Depths* is devoid of true plot, yet it has considerable violence, with beatings and a hanging off-stage and an accidental killing on-stage. Chekhov's character-study *The Cherry Orchard* has no physical action, while his

The Sea Gull has two attempts at suicide off-stage, one a failure, the other successful. The only physical action in *The Little Foxes*—except for a slap—comes when the husband is stricken with a heart attack, and the wife, wishing him to die, makes no move to get his medicine, and we watch him struggle across the stage and fall stricken halfway up the stairs.

"Business" Can Be Fine Theatre

What I have said about subordinating physical action or playing it off-stage does not mean that movement, pantomime, and stage business are not powerful aids to the dramatist. "Show—not tell," said Mark Swan, a popular playwright of many years ago. In the second act of *A Doll's House* the dropping into the letter-box of Krogstad's note exposing Nora's forgery—simple as this business may seem—is one of the most powerful and unforgettable pieces of physical action in modern drama. That letter-box and its threatening secret hang over the rest of the play. Nora's tarantella, designed to distract her husband from the opening of the letter-box and to express her desperation, is another strikingly significant action. This is the stuff of which the best theatre is made. But equally powerful in creating suspense and building the whole pattern of the play are the lines in which Nora tells Mrs. Linde of how she secretly had borrowed money to save her husband's life, and the lines, later on, in which we learn that she had secured the money by forging a note.

J. M. Barrie once said: "The best moments always happen when nobody says anything," and we often feel this in the theatre, but such moments of silence depend on what has been said just before. The thrilling piece of physical action in *The Little Foxes* that I have described is only possible because of the words which fill the scenes before.

All this makes one a little impatient of the dictum: "The skeleton of a play is always a pantomime." Physical action can be electric, but only because of what we know about the characters of the play and their relationships, all of which has to be conveyed by words. A play, as Lawson has said, "cannot be defined as a character or a group of characters," but, though "character is a mode of action which is subsidiary to the whole action," it is nevertheless "a living part of the whole," and to me it is the most important part. For, as someone has said, "Plot is character in action, character seeking the means of asserting itself."

The Theatre Moves Toward Less Physical Action

The theatre of the peaceful world of fifty and sixty years ago—and for some centuries before that—was given far more to violence than the theatre that has known two world wars. (Perhaps the superior "realism" of the movies has saved the stage from reflecting the brute force of our times.) Maeterlinck wrote in 1896, "When I go to the theatre I feel as though I were spending a few hours with my ancestors, who conceived life as something that was primitive, arid, and brutal." Andreyev inquired: "Is action, in the sense of movements and visual achievements on the stage, necessary to the theatre?" He asked this after Ibsen and Chekhov had already shown it was not; but, in the popular theatre of Paris and London, where these Russian and Norwegian playwrights were notable for their absence, the romantic hero still trod the boards, and physical violence was common enough in the so-called triangle plays of infidelity. Unconsciously, Maeterlinck cried out as much against this theatre as against Zola when he wrote: "An old man, seated in his arm-chair, waiting patiently, with his lamp beside him—submitting with bent head to the presence of his soul and his destiny—motionless as he is, does yet live in reality a deeper, more human, and more universal life than the lover who strangles his mistress, the captain who conquers in battle, or the husband who 'avenges his honor.'"

Forty years ago, the American playwright Augustus Thomas demonstrated through a short scene, which I don't think he used in a play, how a character who tells another character certain facts from the past can produce true dramatic action even though neither man moves from his place:

Let us suppose that an old man is standing by the mantelpiece, a young man sitting in a chair. They do not move. The old man is talking of heredity, of what a fine thing it is to have had good parents and grandparents. The young man begins to feel that a family line means much, that he is for that reason all the prouder of his father. Then suppose the older man, never moving, tells the boy that the man of whom he is so proud is not his father. There you get in the boy a violent action, mental yet violent. Then if the old man tells him that he himself is his father, you get another action, of a different sort, and perhaps more violent because of the variety. Yet all the time neither of the men has moved from his position.

Thomas might have cited Arthur Schnitzler's *The Hour of Recognition*, which creates a marked reaction in the audience and on a character by words that are spoken without violence and without movement. A doctor and his wife appear to be a normal, loving couple as they discuss the daughter who has just left for her honeymoon. While the doctor is in his consulting room, another physician says good-bye to the wife before leaving for a war in Asia. From their quiet reminiscences, we learn abruptly that they had been lovers, that she had loved this man better than her husband, and that she had had still another lover. The husband returns, and, after the friend leaves, he and his wife continue their quiet conversation. As he looks through his newspaper, he tells her that she must leave his home. Ten years ago he learned that she had been unfaithful to him. It was with a man of whom he was professionally jealous and at a time when he most needed her love and support. He had ignored the issue because their daughter required a normal home. But now with quiet bitterness he sums up all that she has done to him, and ends their relationship forever.

Action Thrives on Complications

Freytag once wrote: "By action is meant an event or an occurrence arranged according to a controlling idea, and having its meaning made apparent by characters." He might have said that it is what a playwright achieves through the proper interaction of characters. But Freytag would have had to add that the resulting action will be merely narrative unless the playwright gives to the interaction of the characters a dramatic pattern that grows in clarity and intensity throughout the play. I think this can be most easily achieved through injecting complications based on character.

8

Suspense through Complications

. . . if there is no complication and suspense in the action, it cannot be other than a poor play.

GOLDONI

The True Elixir — Complications

As you may have gathered by this time, every theorist of playwriting seeks to find the one vital principle of the art, the single essence of craftmanship, that is the secret of effective dramaturgy. Like the alchemist, he is in quest of the sovereign means, he is seeking the magical formula that will transmute the dross of action into the gold of dramatic success. Though there is almost infinite variety in the thousands upon thousands of plays that have won an audience, though they follow many different patterns and seem to owe their success to many different factors, the theorist still seeks—and finds—the principle, the essence, the rule, the law, that sways and animates them all. One writer finds it in the conflict of two wills, another in unity of action, another in crisis, others in the dominating "premise," the "proposition." I must confess that I am no exception. I, too, have my favorite piece of play-making machinery.

I find only one factor that is common to all plays and sets a play apart from every other form of literary fiction. That factor is complication. It is not of prime importance in *every* play. Its skillful use will not alone save poor material, and make a silken purse out of a sow's ear. But it is present in *all* plays because it is a device which creates the suspense that "holdeth old men from the chimney corner" and keeps them happily affixed to a seat in a theatre. It makes an audience worry—which is the chief purpose of drama so far as technique is concerned.

Suspense is an end, not a means. When Archer doubted that conflict was always and invariably the cause of suspense, he turned to crisis as the explanation. He saw that one crisis was not enough, that the drama was the art of *crises*. One crisis must succeed another. The means, which he did not point out, are complications—not one but many, a new complication to make each new crisis.

More Than One Complication Essential

Lope de Vega wrote: "Do not permit the untying of the plot until reaching the last scene; for the crowd, knowing what the end is, will turn its face to the door and its shoulder to what it has awaited three hours face to face." He might also have said that no simple and single knot in the thread of drama—in other words, no one conflict, no one crisis—can hold an audience in its seat for a whole evening. Playgoers are easily bored; they must be held by mounting suspense. New crises, born of new complications, provide this.

Rowe, who recognizes and emphasizes the power of the complication, points out the need of three basic specimens. First, there is "the complication precipitating the attack," which means the complication that creates the first crisis, the first scene of tension and drama. Next, he lists "the crucial complication," which, I presume, sets off the climactic scene. Last, he speaks of "the resolving complication," which ends the climax and, usually, the play. But Rowe recognizes that there must be many more complications within the plot, each creating a crisis. Complications "are the stuff of which the bulk of the drama structurally is built." A series of complications produces a series of crises, and, of course, the crises must mount in intensity, and all the complications and crises must fit a single, over-all pattern of steadily developing emotional interest.

Complications Must Seem Uncontrived

Since a play must *seem* to move forward without either the assistance or the interference of the author, the complications must not appear to be conveniently dragged in. The course of action must seem logical and self-contained to the very end. Therefore, as

Krows has said, "The sort of action that has to reach out every now and then for an outside complication to keep it going can move only by fits and starts and cannot have full cumulative strength." Complications are actually contrived by the playwright, but he must not let this be evident.

At the beginning of a play, almost anything is possible; the audience grants the author the right to set up in the first act whatever materials he may need. After the first act, he introduces important new material at his peril; he may safely do so only if he takes pains to make it seem to fit in with the developing pattern of the play. If he is wise, he will foreshadow the material in some fashion by introducing earlier in the play the characters who will later convey it. Nobody objects because Ibsen interrupts the happy Christmas atmosphere of the first act of *A Doll's House* to let us know that Nora has deceived her husband by secretly borrowing money. The audience is not upset—except emotionally, which is most desirable—when it learns within the last ten minutes of the act that Nora had committed a forgery to get the money. If these complications had suddenly cropped out in the second or the third acts, however, the audience would have rebelled at such contrivances. The influence that Mrs. Linde and Dr. Rank have on the course of the second and third acts of *A Doll's House* is readily accepted because they were introduced earlier in the play—as a matter of fact, in the first act.

Romeo and Juliet gives us interesting examples of complications, both good and bad. The first, of course, is that the son and the daughter of two feuding families fall in love on a chance meeting at a ball. The next complication—when Romeo hears Juliet confessing to the stars that she loves him—is sheer wilful accident helped by an overheard soliloquy; but this obvious contrivance comes soon enough to make us accept it. Shakespeare then throws an added difficulty in the way of the secretly married lovers by having Romeo kill Tybalt, a cousin of Juliet. This complication is most ingeniously handled. In the very first scene of the play the Prince of Verona has banned all brawls between the rival families on pain of death. In the second scene the author has established the fiery Tybalt as hating Romeo for his intrusion at the ball. Shakespeare makes the killing of Tybalt doubly acceptable: first he has Romeo try to avoid a duel with his new kinsman; next, he allows impetuous Mercutio to take the quarrel on himself and be slain; only then does the playwright let Romeo come to blows with Tybalt and kill him. This complication causes the banishment of Romeo. The next is the decision of Juliet's parents to marry her to Paris, already foreshadowed in the second scene of the play. Following this, Shakespeare brings in the potent drug—as preposterous as it is unprepared for—that will stop the wedding by making Juliet appear, for a time, to be dead. Friar Lawrence writes a letter to Romeo in Mantua telling him to return to Verona and rescue Juliet from the tomb, but—and here comes the worst sort of complication, because it is mere accident—the letter miscarries and Romeo hears only of Juliet's death and burial. Resolving complications rapidly ensue. Romeo encounters and kills Paris at the tomb. He drinks poison over Juliet's body. She awakes too late, and stabs herself. Peace between the Capulets and the Montagues!

Watch carefully in all the plays you see or read, and you will find that complications play a vital part. In a rare few—*The Cherry Orchard* and *The Lower Depths,* for instance—they may be very slight. *Liliom* has only one more than the major three that Rowe prescribed. The "precipitating complication" is that Julie and not Marie decides to stay overnight with Liliom. The "crucial complication"—a double one—is that Liliom, learning he is to be a father, decides on a robbery and bungles it. The final "resolving complication" is that Liliom, true to his nature, slaps his little daughter instead of doing her a kindness, and goes back to hell, while his wife tells us at last—in one of the most beautiful, touching, and significant last lines of any play—of how she has always loved and understood Liliom.

THE CHILD: —tell me—has it ever happened to you—has anyone ever hit you—without hurting you in the least?

JULIE: Yes, my child. It has happened to me, too.

[*There is a pause.*]

THE CHILD: Is it possible for someone to hit you —hard like that—real loud and hard—and not hurt you at all?

JULIE: It is possible, dear—that someone may beat you and beat you and beat you—and not hurt you at all—

Sometimes complications are purely mechanical, though within the bounds of plausibility—as, for instance, the orders to move up to the fighting front that twice arrive conveniently in *What Price Glory?*. In *Ah, Wilderness!* a few complications move the plot ahead a bit, but they are relatively unimportant compared with the author's pleasant and observant vaudeville of human nature at the turn of the century.

Very rarely, complications develop from new characters. In Galsworthy's *Escape* only the character of the convict who breaks prison runs throughout the play, and his encounter with each new group of people brings a fresh complication, while some of the episodes carry small complications for the other characters. In the fourth scene, at the inn, and in the last two, at the home of the spinsters and at the church, the entrances of various people produce fine suspense through intricate complications.

The "Obligatory Scene"

There has been a good deal of twaddle about the discovery by Francisque Sarcey, the French critic, of the "*scène a faire*," which Archer translated as the "obligatory scene." This is a scene that is supposed to be made absolutely necessary by the general pattern of the plot. According to Archer it is one "which the audience (more or less clearly and consciously) foresees and desires, and the absence of which it may with reason resent." The playgoer is supposed to look forward to the big clash between hero and villian. Actually, the obligatory scene is seldom accurately anticipated. In student work it is sometimes discovered or recognized through its absence. The obligatory scene is almost invariably produced by a complication. It is put off by other complications; if this were not so, the play would be over in fifteen minutes. In *Hamlet* the obligatory scene is postponed through the whole play and it comes about only because the King plots clumsily the murder of the hero. In *A Doll's House* it is a quite unexpected scene that results from the husband's saying in the last act, "Nora, I am saved!" instead of, "Nora, you are saved!"

Surprise and Suspense United in a Complication

There has also been a good deal of talk about suspense versus surprise, and here, too, the complication is important. Surprise, while arresting and exciting, is never as valuable, generally speaking, as suspense. Surprise is gone with the wind, while suspense lives on and on. The Greeks valued surprise highly in their "peripeties," their scenes where—usually because of word brought by a messenger—the fortunes of the hero were completely reversed. But since their day surprise has fallen into disfavor as a dramatic device. Synge must have smiled a little superiorly when he read a letter in which Yeats wrote, "Surprise . . . is what is necessary. Surprise, and then more surprise, and that is all." Yeats should have read Schlegel: "Whoever is struck down in a moment, I can only pity for the moment. But how if I expect the blow, how if I see the storm brewing for some time about my head or his?"

I mention surprise versus suspense at this point only because a complication usually carries both values, and in a complication surprise is most commonly and successfully used. The first effect of a complication is the shock of the unexpected. The next—which follows immediately—is enduring and rewarding suspense, suspense that carries the play on until the next shock is necessary.

In another chapter I have spoken of the "strong curtain," a theatrical custom more honored in the breach, these days, than in the observance. The surprise of complication is usually the basis of a strong curtain-line. Modern plays seldom begin or end with such powerful complications as the appearance of the Ghost in *Hamlet* or the exchange of the "unbated and envenom'd" foil and the Queen's drinking from the poisoned cup. As a matter of fact, Shakespeare did not bring down his curtain on the deaths of Laertes, Gertrude, Claudius, and Hamlet. A playwright like Scribe or Sardou would have gone for such a curtain.

The "Three-Legged" Stool

There is a very ingenious form of complication which is so rare that, if used at all, it is almost certain to be used for a strong curtain. An old form of this occurs in a play of Scribe's. Discussing the responsibilities of the confessional, a middle-aged priest in a small town tells a casual acquaintance that the first man he confessed revealed he was a murderer. An important character in the play—a man of the priest's own age who had left the town and made his fortune in Paris—now enters, and in the course of conversation, says to the priest's friend something like this: "I have a very warm feeling for Father Jean, for when he was a young priest and had just come here to this parish, I was the first man he confessed."

Augustus Thomas once described this device as the "three-legged stool." An audience is given two facts; then it learns a third, and, by a sort of miracle, it finds a new and surprising structure standing before it. Thomas cited the end of the first act of William C. De Mille's play of some forty years ago *The Woman.* The scene is a hotel lobby in Washington. A reactionary political boss and his son-in-law, once a governor of New York and now a representative in Congress, are discussing a young, liberal congressman named

Standish who is making trouble for their "interests." The boss says that he has learned that the congressman had an affair a few years ago with a woman who later married someone else. They plan to learn the name of the woman and use this to make him vote as they wish. The boss tells Standish what they know, hoping he will betray the woman by trying to warn her. When the boss has left the lobby Standish hurriedly puts through a long-distance call to New York; he asks for an odd and easily-remembered number—Plaza 1001. Within a dozen speeches the former governor returns to the lobby to telephone his wife. He calls Plaza 1001.

The "three-legged stool" is an obvious device and very difficult to work out, but if it can be used at all, it is most effective. If you are writing a serious drama, you must be careful that its use does not seem a mere piece of theatricalism. It should be employed subtly and discreetly.

Dramatic vs. Narrative Writing

The difference between dramatic and narrative writing has not, I think, been completely or effectively explained. For two years I tried earnestly and not very successfully to convey it to my playwriting classes. Then I found what I think is the key to the matter.

There are certain very obvious and superficial differences. For example, it is harder to write good plays than good novels. Bernard Shaw had some fun with Arnold Bennett when he was rash enough to observe that "one reason why a play is easier to write than a novel" is because "a play is shorter than a novel." Shaw replied "It is; and so is the *Bible* shorter than the *London Directory*. 'Excuse the length of my letter,' said Pascal, 'I had no time to write a short one.'" Shaw then took the nine speeches and 278 words of the scene between Macbeth and Macduff in the last act of *Macbeth*—"one of the shortest, most intense, and most famous scenes in English dramatic literature"—and turned it into twenty-five hundred words "in the style of my friends Bennett and Wells and Galsworthy," which really became a happy burlesque.

The important difference is not, of course, that a play is shorter or more condensed or harder to write, or that a novel may have long descriptions, dozens or even hundreds of characters, philosophizings by the author as well as the characters, or that it may be written in the first person, simply and directly or through the "stream of consciousness" technique.

The difference is partly that, because the play is shorter, it must pack more of plot and character into fewer words, and, because it is thus in danger of overtaxing and confusing an audience that cannot stop and think or read over again, the play must have greater immediate clarity and the plot must be presented with much more unity.

Archer got nearer the mark when he wrote: "The drama may be called the art of crisis, as fiction is the art of gradual developments." Archer came still closer with this: "Most great novels embrace considerable segments of many lives; whereas the drama gives us only the culminating points—or shall we say the intersecting culminations?—two or three destinies."

The secret lies in those words "intersecting culminations." They mean the effect of one life or one character upon another. "Culminations" sounds as if we had reached the last third or perhaps the very end-climax of a play. But by looking at many, many plays from *Oedipus* to *The Death of a Salesman* you will see that a drama is usually so condensed and so unified in action and often in time that the "intersecting" of lives at any point in a play does indeed come close to the "culminations" of those lives so far as their existence in the theatre is concerned.

This is a rather special and highbrow way of getting around to my real point about the dramatic versus the narrative. I used to try to describe the unique form of a play as a story that is like the wheel of a car moving forward, with one point on the circumference bounding up and ahead and coming to earth again in a series of arcs of movement. I used to try to show that a plot spun ahead in more and more rapid and complex gyrations with a succession of new forces whipping it on. All the time, I was looking for something that is implied in Archer's "intersecting culminations" and is actually made concrete in the word "complications."

Novels have complications, of course, but the novel does not depend on them as does the drama. Again the reason is the greater condensation of the play and the greater necessity for packing more material and more exciting material into a smaller space of time and action.

Complications play a more or less important part in all plays; they are the life-blood of 99⁹⁹⁄₁₀₀ per cent of them. Examine for yourself *The Death of a Salesman* and see how complications out of the past or forming in the present appear, press forward, and pile up to seal—and to explain—the fate of Willy Loman. Apply the same sort of analysis to *All My Sons, Born Yesterday, State of the Union, Watch on the Rhine, The Philadelphia Story, Mourning Becomes Electra, The Swan, Leah Kleschna, Sag Harbor, The School for Scandal, Tartuffe, Twelfth Night,* and back to *Oedipus,* and you will see how steadily and completely the use of complications stamps the drama for its own.

Test your own play to see if it has enough complications. At the end of each scene or act, ask yourself whether the audience will be worrying and what it will be worrying about. If it will not be worrying at all, or if it will be worrying about something not very important, then you need a new complication, something really worth worrying over.

Ibsen's Consummate Use of Complications

My sense of the prime importance of the complication came through reading and seeing Ibsen's *A Doll's House* once more just a few years ago. I suppose it could have been one of a number of other plays that I might have read or seen at the time, but it was Ibsen's elaborate and consummate use of the complication that made me conscious of the determining part it plays in the dramatic form. Let me analyze the first act to let you see how complication works:

The scene opens on a happy family at Christmas. A Victorian family: Nora, a wife treated as a charming doll, Torvald, a dominant and handsome husband full of budgetary caution though he has just been made manager of a bank. Enter a widow, an old and long-absent friend of Nora's, Mrs. Linde, and we learn the following facts. At the start of Nora's marriage, her husband had been desperately ill, and had had to go to a warmer climate to recover. The doctor said Torvald should not be alarmed by being told the truth, so Nora had to borrow the money for the trip secretly and without her husband's consent—an illegal proceeding at that time. Here is the first complication, for Torvald will be furious if he finds out. We learn that a dubious character named Krogstad, whom Mrs. Linde once knew, has a job in the bank, and that Torvald will give Mrs. Linde a position there. Krogstad enters and we find that he is the man from whom Nora borrowed the money. We learn further that he fears he may lose his job to Mrs. Linde or through Torvald's former antagonism toward him. With a covert threat he presses Nora to protect him in his job. This complication is topped by Krogstad's exposure to the audience that Nora forged her dead father's signature as security for the loan. "If I lose my position . . . you shall lose yours with me." Re-enter Torvald, who has seen Krogstad leave. At first Nora denies his visit. Upon her admission that he has been there and just as she begins a plea for Krogstad, Torvald says he will discharge the man, reads her a moral lecture on the evil influence a deceitful mother may have on her children—which, he says, had accounted for Krogstad's "fall"—and asserts his complete aversion to anyone guilty of deceit. Nora learns, thereby, how unstable her happy marriage is: Krogstad has threatened to expose her forgery, yet, if this danger is averted, she will be living a deceit and be unfit to mother her children. Not yet abjuring the soliloquy, Ibsen ends the act with Nora crying: "No, no—it isn't true. It's impossible; it must be impossible. [She tells the nurse not to bring in her children.] It's not true. It can't possibly be true."

With these complications exposed—dramatic in themselves and full of suspense—with this material at hand, Ibsen goes on to build three more acts of mounting complications and added suspense. Take away the complications, and the story of *A Doll's House*—the story of a wife who discovers she is a puppet and a plaything, not an equal partner in marriage—could still be told, but it would not be a play.

Not all plays are so articulated as *A Doll's House*, with the menace of past events exposed in the present, but none of them can live without this stuff of which drama is made. Complication stamps the dramatic form with its own peculiar pattern. Mastering the use of complication is the hardest task that faces the student, but it is the most rewarding. If he has no talent for the devising of complications, he had better give up playwriting.

9

The Writing

From Scenario through Dialogue

Technical skill is like a motor car; it can take you where you want to go but it can't tell you where to go.

ALAN THOMPSON

Plan Before You Write

THE GREATEST MISTAKE YOU CAN MAKE AS A BEGINning playwright is to plunge into dialogue with only a general idea of where you are going. Even if you know the main characters you want to use, what your first scene is going to be, some situations on the way to the climax, and the end of your play, you are not far enough along to start writing your first draft. Before you put down a word of dialogue you should have a complete outline that covers every scene in your play, a scenario worked out in as much detail as possible.

"The skeleton," said Archer, "is, in a sense, the fundamental element in the human organism. It can exist, and, with a little assistance, retain its form, when stripped of muscle and blood and nerve, whereas a boneless man would be an amorphous heap, more helpless than a jellyfish. . . . The scenario, or skeleton, is so manifestly the natural groundwork of a dramatic performance that the playwrights of the Italian *commedia dell' arte* wrote nothing more than a scheme of scenes, and left the actors to do the rest."

A play needs a skeleton because a play is almost as complex as the human body. A story may contain a suitable plot, but the plot has to be arranged and organized in the greatest detail before you can know if it will make an effective play. It is only through a full scenario that you can test whether you are putting together a plot that will mount steadily in dramatic interest, keep your audience worrying over the troubles of your characters, and end in emotional satisfaction.

If you start writing before you have worked out your action in detail, you will discover, to your sorrow, how much more complex a play is than you ever imagined. When you have finished the first act and got well into the second, you will find that you have to go back and change scene after scene in your first act. You may find that you are miles off the path of your plot, or that something you want a character to do or say in the second act contradicts something you have had him do or say in the first. A new and exciting scene may come into your head that requires the complete revision of your plot-line up to that point. Robert Ardrey, author of *Thunder Rock*, told me of encountering just such troubles when he wrote his first play, *Star Spangled,* without having worked out a scenario. He wrote the first act thirteen times, the second act nine times, and the last act three times. Without proper planning, the job of revision will seem almost endless, and it will be devitalizing to the script and heartbreaking to the writer.

The beginner who objects to developing a scenario usually rationalizes his laziness by saying that it will destroy his spontaneity and imagination. It may do so to a very small extent, but this is negligible compared with the greater dramatic force and the saving in ultimate work that result from planning carefully every scene in a play. As a playwright grows more adept he may find that he can work from a less detailed outline; he may even find that he has to put down on paper only the major characters and the sequence of scenes, carrying in his head quite a lot of detail and evolving the rest as he goes along. Successful playwrights work in different ways, but they have all developed some definite means of holding their plots in line. Back in the eighteenth century Goldoni outlined his own method: "The first step was the making of an outline with its division into the three principle parts: the exposition, the arch of the plot, and the catastrophe. The second step consisted of the apportioning of the action among acts and scenes; the third in the dialoging of the most interesting incidents; the fourth in the general dialoging of the whole."

Later, he confessed, he was able to combine the steps of this operation, but that was only when he had reached the summit of his powers—after writing how many of his 1800 plays?

Making a scenario does not mean that everything becomes frozen. The scenario itself will be rewritten and reorganized as new ideas and situations develop. In the dialoging, too, you will find opportunities for improving your outline. Ibsen himself made a lot of important alterations as he wrote and rewrote. This is obvious in the volume of earlier and later drafts called *From Ibsen's Workshop.* He had done a good deal of work on *Rosmersholm* before he decided that Rebecca West should not be married to Rosmer, and that Rosmer should not have two grown daughters. Archer believes that when Ibsen set up the past relations of Krogstad and Mrs. Linde in *A Doll's House* in such a fashion that they could fall in love again in the last act and remove the threat of exposure of Nora's forgery, the playwright had in mind a happy ending of mutual adjustment. But, if he did, this was before he had finished the first draft.

A play should, as Archer has said, "be kept fluid or plastic as long as possible, and not suffered to become immutably fixed, either in the author's mind or on paper, before it has had time to grow and ripen." But, for the beginner, this means working long and arduously over the scenario, not starting on the dialogue with a plot that is shapeless and wandering.

The scenario can take a number of different forms. In any case you need to set down the order of the scenes between your characters and what happens in each of them in terms of what your characters do and say. A rather elaborate but effective form is to list, in three columns, certain facts about each scene. In the first, the names of the characters, in the second, the essence of what they are to do or say, and then, in the third, a summary of what the scene accomplishes in terms of character establishment, exposition, complication, conflict, suspense, or resolution.

The Need for Preparation

In your scenario you must be careful to indicate where you need lines or situations that prepare for later action. Though mere preparation carries no dramatic excitement, it is most important if the audience is to understand and accept later actions of characters. Examine any play and you will find innumerable examples. Sometimes it is as simple as the talk in the first act of *A Doll's House* indicating that Dr. Rank is on intimate terms with the family, and the query almost at the start of *Riders to the Sea,* "Is the sea bad by the white rocks?" Or it may be as elaborate as the way John Van Druten prepares us to accept Sally's affair with the soldier in *The Voice of the Turtle.* As Miss Gallaway points out:

Van Druten carefully contrasts Sally with Olive, a lady of definitely easy virtue. Sally is shocked and repentant at her own love life, which is represented as meager. She is determined never to have another *affaire*. She is practically trapped by a severe rainstorm and the crowded conditions of New York hotels into lending her day bed to a soldier on leave. Only after we are convinced that Sally is at heart a nice home-town girl does Van Druten allow her to bring out of her own bureau drawer her ex-lover's pyjamas, an act which is in itself an evidence of her naïveté.

Krows, who calls preparation "the great dramatic principle known wherever there is dramatic art," gives an interesting example of its effectiveness in Edward Knoblock's play of forty years ago, *Discovering America:*

. . . the servant, Ernesto, kisses the ring of the Cardinal when the latter speaks to him. No spectator expects from that more than the authentic business it seems to be; but it really is preparation for the subsequent introduction of Miss Dix to the Cardinal. At that time the Cardinal holds out his hand to this young lady, and to his amazement and brief indignation, she shakes it instead of kissing the ring. Without the preparation the entire point of this would have been lost on many persons in the audience.

In Sidney Howard's *Yellow Jack* there is a clear example of a failure to prepare properly. During the last five minutes of the play there is a scene in which one of two soldiers who have voluntarily exposed themselves to the bite of the yellow-fever-carrying mosquito feels the first indications of the disease. Howard wanted to introduce the lines from Shakespeare that begin: "Cowards die many times before their death." So he calmly and obviously had the sickening soldier say to his friend: "You wouldn't like to speak some Shakespeare for me?" Realizing that the audience would be surprised to discover that the friend had a Shakespearean repertory, Howard hastily tried to alibi the matter by having the sick man add: "You usually like to when there's nobody around." As this scene is part of the climax of the play, it is the worst possible time to risk pulling the audience out of emotional illusion with a lame excuse for a recitation. Howard could easily have planted earlier in the play the soldier's fondness for spouting Shakespeare, and could even have got some characterizing comedy out of it.

Sometimes it is necessary to prepare for the use of properties, especially important ones. Augustus Thomas explained this very carefully in connection with a weapon used to kill a man in *The Witching Hour:*

> A dagger would have been too lethal, would have startled the audience too much. So a two-foot, ivory paperknife from my own desk served instead. Then the audience had to learn three things about it: Its position, its purpose, its ability to kill. The first two were accomplished by having a girl pick it up to cut a magazine; the third, by a

woman's knocking it to the floor where it made a resounding thump.

Ibsen was most skillful in the matter of the pistol with which Hedda Gabler killed herself. He introduced it at the beginning of act two, when she playfully discharges it into the garden as Judge Brack approaches. Later, she presents it to Eilert Lovborg so that he may kill himself. Brack's discovery that Lovborg's death was caused by Hedda's pistol provides him with the hold over her that is a contributing motive to her own suicide. Moreover, the pistol is one of a pair that make up the only inheritance left to Hedda from her father's estate; they symbolize her physical bankruptcy.

It is usually wise to prepare for the entrances of important characters, and it is always necessary to provide a reason, as, for instance, to return something borrowed, to pay a friendly visit, to collect a debt or renew an acquaintance. Getting a character off the stage when he is not wanted sometimes requires preparation. Ibsen was not always careful to provide it. In *A Doll's House*, when Nora sees Torvald approaching and wants to be alone with him, she tells Mrs. Linde, who is sewing, to leave the room because "Torvald can't bear to see dressmaking going on." In *Rosmersholm*, Rebecca West gets rid of Mrs. Hilseth by saying that Rosmer "doesn't like to see dusting going on." Both speeches seem lame excuses. It would have looked less obvious if Ibsen had planted in earlier scenes the peculiar attitudes of his heroes toward dressmaking and dusting.

Be careful to account for lapses of time in realistic plays. If a character has to go to the mail box or over to the drugstore, don't let him come back too soon, and be sure to fill his absence with talk that moves the plot ahead.

Names and Settings

Take pains over the names of your characters. Don't risk confusion by naming one Stanley and another Stanhope. I have had a student call one boy Joe and another Joey. Don't call a hobo Eric Stuyvesant or a poet Bill Higgins unless you want the name to indicate something out of his past. For the hero of *A School for Scandal,* Sheridan considered Clerimont, Florival, Captain Harry Plausible, Harry Pliant, Harry Pliable, Young Harrier, and Frank before he settled on Charles Surface. Ibsen discarded Stenborg ("Stonecastle") for Helmer in *A Doll's House* because he decided it had too burlesque a flavor. The names Quirt and Flagg seem just as right for the battling heroes of *What Price Glory?* as does Falder for the doomed man in *Justice.* Morrell has the proper moral flavor for Shaw's clergyman in *Candida,* and Prossy conveys the somewhat prissy flavor of his secretary.

Give the reader a full description of your characters,

for the reader may turn out to be a producer or a director. And put these descriptions into the script where you first introduce the people. They will help to visualize them almost as much as the actors who finally play the parts.

Either describe your sets and their furniture fully and clearly or leave them largely to the reader's imagination. It is best to provide simple ground plans. That will make the action easier to follow and prevent you from having too many doors on one side of the room. Don't plan your sets in the splayed-out fashion of the scenery of forty years ago, with side walls slanting in toward the rear of the stage. In a properly rectangular set, the up-stage corners will be invisible to those of the audience who sit far to the right or left, but you can fill those areas with jogs or walled-in closets or stairs, or with large pieces of furniture. Often the corner of a room set diagonally on the stage is very effective. Don't ask for the interior of a cathedral when a side aisle and a pillar will do just as well, both for acting space and as a suggestion of atmosphere.

Stage Directions

In describing entrances and exits avoid the stage jargon of the past such as "R. 1. E" or "runs across stage R. U. E. to L. D. E." Say "John enters from the hall door" or "Ethel crosses hastily from the dining-

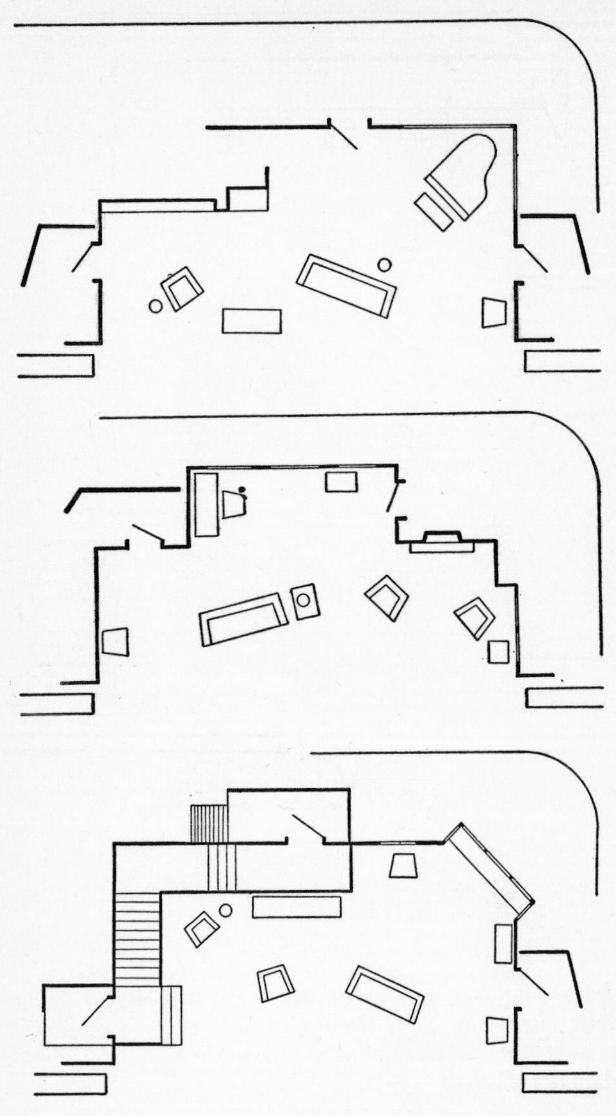

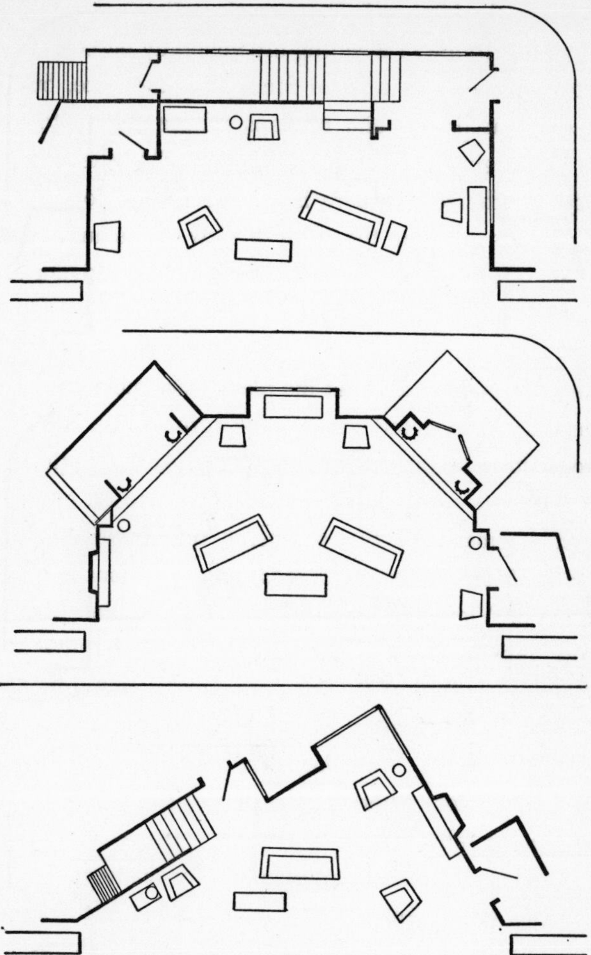

Plans of rectangular sets, showing various methods of filling up-stage corners with jogs or large props, and the diagonal placing of a set. The thin black line above each set represents the back-drop or cyclorama.

room to the kitchen." The directions "left" and "right" in a description of a setting are generally based on the point of view of an actor facing the audience, but it is quite as proper and perhaps a little clearer to say at the beginning something like this: "At the left, as you see the room, there is a large couch," or "Stage directions are from the point of view of the audience."

Shaw was one of the first playwrights to give a natural and even a literary flavor to the descriptions of sets and characters and to stage directions—perhaps because he realized that his plays were more likely to be read than acted around the turn of the century. Sometimes he pushed this rather far. At the beginning of *Candida* he gave about 1500 words to an account that begins with the northeast suburb of London where Morrell's house stands, tells us about the 217 acres of Victoria Park, and the front garden, porch, and steps of the parsonage, and finally describes the drawing room and its furniture, books, pictures, and people. Yet, however over-elaborate Shaw sometimes was in his stage directions, they proved of inestimable aid to directors wherever the playwright could not be present at rehearsals.

Barrie, who resisted publication for many years, got obvious enjoyment out of describing his settings and his characters as elaborately and amusingly as he would have done if he had been writing a novel. (Often he was annoyingly "cute" about it.) He devoted a thousand words to introducing the setting and first three characters of *Alice Sit-by-the-Fire,* beginning with: "One would like to peep covertly into Amy's diary (octavo, with the word 'Amy' in gold letters wandering across the soft brown leather covers, as if it were a long word and, in Amy's opinion, rather a dear)." He began *The Admirable Crichton* with: "A moment before the curtain rises, the Hon. Ernest Woolley drives up to the door of Loam House in Mayfair. There is a happy smile on his pleasant, insignificant face, and this presumably means that he is thinking of himself." After opening *The Twelve-Pound Look* with: "If quite convenient (as they say about cheques) you are to consider that the scene is laid in your own house, and that Harry Sims is you." Barrie larded the play with observations such as: "He is too modest to boast about himself, and prefers to keep a wife in the house for that purpose," "She smiles, heaven knows why, unless her next remark explains it," and "looking not unkindly into the soul of this man."

The Art of Exposition

The problem of exposition arises from the fact that you cannot make the action of a play convey all the information needed on the backgrounds of your characters, and on events—very important to the action—that may have happened before the curtain rises or that may happen off-stage. Your characters must convey this information to the audience without seeming to go out of their way to do so. Fortunately, with a little thought and imagination, the art of exposition is not too hard to master.

The Greeks used the Chorus to set up the basis of the play, explain the characters, and cover the antecedent action. Shakespeare used a medieval variant of this in a figure sometimes called Chorus, sometimes Prologue, who appeared upon the stage before the play began; in *Henry V* he gave us thirty-four lines of exposition in this way. Sometimes—and more effectively—Shakespeare used a soliloquy charged with emotion, as in *Richard III.* In *Romeo and Juliet,* after having the Chorus deliver a sonnet needlessly telling the audience about the feud between the Montagues and the Capulets and about the tragic issue of the love story, Shakespeare started the action of the play with a scene of quarreling between the rival families that a less skillful playwright might have left to exposition.

Before the advent of realism, a favorite and most inept way of conveying exposition was for characters to tell each other facts they already knew. The "confidant"—a favorite device of the French and English seventeenth-century drama, designed to eliminate the soliloquy—lent a ready ear to the hero's or the heroine's inmost thoughts as well as to his or her recounting of what had gone on before the curtain went up. In *The Critic* Sheridan satirized the breed by having a confidant in white satin go mad at the same time as the heroine. I can still remember farces that began with a butler and a maid who conveyed such information as: "The young master got in very late last night and left his key in the door. If he doesn't mend his ways, his rich aunt will disinherit him, and then the actress Mlle. Fifi will have no more to do with him."

Another device, still in use, is to introduce a stranger, someone who is not familiar with the other characters in the play or who has been out of town for some time. Anna Cora Mowatt's *Fashion,* the first play by an American woman, began with a dialogue between a French maid in the home of the rich Mrs. Tiffany, and a newly hired Negro servant:

ZEKE: I tell 'ee what, Missy, I'm 'stordinary glad to find dis a bery 'spectable situation. Now as you've made de acquaintance of dis here family, and dere you've had a supernumerary advantage ob me—seeing as I only receibed my appointment dis morning. What I wants to know is your publicated opinion, privately expressed, ob de domestic circle.

MILLINETTE: You mean vat *espèce,* vat kind of personnes are Monsieur and Madame Tiffany? Ah! Monsieur is not de same ting as Madame, not at all.

ZEKE: I s'pose he ain't altogether.

MILLINETTE: Monsieur is man of business,—Madame is lady of fashion. Monsieur make the money,—Madame spend it. Monsieur nobody at all,—Madame everybody all together. . . .

ZEKE: Well, now we've disposed ob de heads ob de family, who comes next?

MILLINETTE: First, dere is Mademoiselle Seraphina Tiffany. Mademoiselle is not at all one proper *personne.* Mademoiselle Seraphina is one coquette.

The Aside and the Soliloquy

The aside was another method frequently employed for exposition, sometimes for comedy effect. In *Fashion,* a bogus French count has the following dialogue with Mrs. Tiffany:

MRS. TIFFANY: You, Count, I presume, are at home in all the courts of Europe.

COUNT JOLIMAITRE: *Courts?* Eh? Oh, yes, madame, very true. I believe I am pretty well known in some of the courts of Europe—[*aside*] police courts.

Another purveyor of information was the soliloquy. Just as Snake, in the first scene of *A School for Scandal,* informs Lady Sneerwell of facts that would seem far better known to her than to him, Sir Peter Teazle comes on alone in the second scene to tell himself and the audience all about his marriage. At the end of the first act of *Othello* Shakespeare gave Iago twenty-one lines of soliloquy in which to make clear his own villainous nature and the substance of his plot against the Moor. In *The People's Lawyer,* an American play of 1839, Charles, the honest clerk, seizes a moment of privacy to observe:

He knows not of my poverty or he would not have asked me to go to a ball or wonder at my refusal. Daily, sums of gold and silver pass through my hands sufficient to purchase splendor and independence—yet not mine. Nightly do I go to a home where poverty is ever present and distress may suddenly come with a temptation to use what is another's. The evil one shall not overtake me; I can bear my privations. I will be honest.

Both the aside and the soliloquy were frank, "unnatural" ways of conveying one sort of information or another, but they differed a good deal in technique and purpose. The aside was always injected during a scene of dialogue. It generally conveyed only the shallow and the obvious. The soliloquy was usually delivered to an empty stage, though occasionally, as in the balcony scene in *Romeo and Juliet,* it was overheard. When used by playwrights of stature, its purpose was to present the inner thoughts of a character, the deep emotional doubts or convictions that could find no outlet in ordinary dialogue. In the seventeenth century the Abbé d'Aubinac wrote, in *La pratique du théâtre,* "It is sometimes very pleasant to see a man upon the Stage lay open his heart and speak boldly of his most secret thoughts, explain his designs, and give a vent to all his passion suggests." It was the nobler use of soliloquy that Shakespeare practiced in *Hamlet.* O'Neill gave the aside the emotional and reflective quality of the soliloquy when he began to experiment with it in *The Great God Brown* and made it the dramatic heart of *Strange Interlude.*

At least twice in *A Doll's House,* and also in *Ros-*

mersholm, Ibsen used short soliloquies, some of which may, perhaps, be excused as sudden emotional outpourings. Usually, however, he managed exposition of emotion and fact with consummate skill. Where Scribe and later practitioners of the "well-made play" followed the older pattern of devoting the first act to exposition—true also, to some extent, of *The Little Foxes*—Ibsen spread exposition throughout his plays. Beginning notably in *A Doll's House,* he used it not only to convey simple facts but also to provide dramatic complications.

Sometimes there is little that needs to be exposed to get a play going or to keep it in motion. Maxwell Anderson has to explain very little past action in *Elizabeth the Queen* except that Elizabeth and Essex have quarreled, which he tells us at the start through dialogue between two soldiers. Often, however, there is a great deal of earlier action to be told, and in handling this you should follow the pattern of Ibsen and distribute the exposition throughout the drama, as it is needed. Otherwise you will be in danger of spending most of your first act in describing what Ervine calls "expired" events, and boring your audiences by "giving them descriptions and reminiscences instead of drama."

Various Methods of Exposition

You will find excellent examples of exposition throughout the history of the drama, though playwrights have taken more pains over this matter since the advent of realism. Molière established Tartuffe as a hypocrite without descending to the use of the soliloquy, as did Shakespeare to tell us that Iago was a villain. In *The Emperor Jones* O'Neill uses a terrified servant to tell the white trader that the Negro's followers have run away to the hills, and the playwright brings out in quite natural talk between Jones and the trader the past of the Pullman porter turned emperor. In *All My Sons* Arthur Miller uses the enthusiasm of a neighbor for horoscopes to bring out facts about the boy who was killed in action; without any such device he handles most skillfully the past of the girl who returns to town after a two years' absence. In *Mourning Becomes Electra* O'Neill employs a garrulous old gardener, some townsfolk, and a visiting cousin to explain the story of the dead Mannons and the characters of those living; it is an obvious device, but it sets forth with a certain dramatic significance the special place of the family and their house in the community. In memory, most playgoers who have seen *Our Town* think that Thornton Wilder used the "Stage Manager"—a rural type himself—to tell us about the past history of the people of the play, but actually, although he talks a great deal, he confines himself largely to describing the missing scenery and bridging the changes from scene to scene.

One of the best examples of skillful exposition is found in the opening minutes of *Rosmersholm*. Through comparing the earlier drafts of the play that are printed in *From Ibsen's Workshop* with the final version, you can see how the playwright perfected the scene. The story of why Mrs. Rosmer killed herself is slowly developed throughout the play; in the first scene Ibsen wanted merely to prepare us for the news that she had died by throwing herself from the footbridge into the mill pond, and that Pastor Rosmer has not yet recovered from the blow. In the first version Rosmer (then called Boldt-Romer) asks Rebecca West (then Miss Radeck) where his daughters are, and learns they are skating on the mill pond.

REBECCA: Oh, there's no danger at all. It's not so deep, and besides, the ice is perfectly safe.

ROSMER: I know that; it isn't *that* I was thinking of.

REBECCA: I see, it's on account of—the other thing?

ROSMER: Yes. I think there is something uncanny in the children skating and playing and making a noise just over the spot that was their mother's death-bed.

In the next draft Ibsen improved the exposition considerably, but it is still a bit obvious. The old servant is talking with Rebecca West:

MADAME HELSETH: I suppose I had better begin to lay the tea-table, ma'am?

REBECCA: Yes, please do. He must soon be in now.

MADAME HELSETH: No, he won't come in just yet; for I saw him from the kitchen—

REBECCA: Yes, yes—

MADAME HELSETH: —on the other side of the mill-pond. At first he was going straight across the foot-bridge; but then he turned back—

REBECCA: Did he?

MADAME HELSETH: Yes, and then he went all the way round. Ah, it's strange about such places. A place where a thing like that has happened—there . . . It stays there; it isn't forgotten so soon.

In the last draft Ibsen handled the matter perfectly:

MADAME HELSETH: I suppose I had better begin to lay the table, Miss?

REBECCA WEST: Yes, please do. The Pastor must soon be in now.

MADAME HELSETH: Don't you feel the draught, Miss, where you're sitting?

REBECCA: Yes, there is a little draught. Perhaps you had better shut the window.

MADAME HELSETH [*about to shut the window, looks out*]: Why, isn't that the Pastor over there?

REBECCA: Where? [*Rises*] Yes, it is he. [*Behind the curtain.*] Stand aside—don't let him see us.

MADAME HELSETH: Only think, Miss—he's beginning to use the path by the mill again.

REBECCA: He went that way day before yesterday, too. But let us see whether . . .

MADAME HELSETH: Will he venture across the footbridge?

REBECCA: That is what I want to see. No, he is turning. He is going by the upper road again. A long way round.

MADAME HELSETH: Dear Lord, yes. No wonder the Pastor thinks twice about setting foot on that bridge. A place where a thing like that has happened . . .

In this scene the point to note is not merely the skill with which Ibsen makes the two women talk naturally and plausibly while giving us information. It is not the device of looking out of the window, for that would seem obvious and convenient. It is the fact that Ibsen makes looking out the window appear natural by having the maid ask if Rebecca feels a draught, and then go to close the window. Ibsen uses the window deliberately, but he introduces it through an independent and commonplace incident. Starting exposition by a line or a piece of business "one step removed" from what you want to tell is something to study and to learn to do.

The secret of good exposition in the ordinary course of dialogue is to avoid the direct statement and provide the information obliquely. As an example consider two lines from a student's play and how they could be reworked. As written, the speeches went:

CORPORAL FACE: Yuh see, Sarge, I always wanted to be a detective, and now here's my chance to do some real work with all these crooks in Vienna. Maybe I could even find the Kleffner diamonds. Gee!

SERGEANT JOHNNY: You mean the $200,000 job that's supposed to be dumped round here some place? You're mad. The stuff's out of the country long ago.

It is not at all difficult to rewrite the last speech so that the sergeant gives us the facts without being obvious:

SERGEANT JOHNNY: Aw, you're nuts. No thief would leave $200,000 worth of loot around here. The stuff's out of the country long ago.

To letters, which were once a handy vehicle of exposition, modern science and industry have added the telephone, the dictaphone, and the stenographer. These give a character many an excuse for getting convenient facts off his mind and into the minds of the audience.

At the beginning of *The Play's the Thing*, Molnar—always a *bravura* as well as a skillful writer—reduces exposition to the terms of pure "theatre":

MANSKY: What's on your mind, Sandor?

TURAI: I was just thinking how extraordinarily difficult it is to begin a play. The eternal problem of how to introduce your principal characters.

ADAM: I suppose it must be hard.

TURAI: It is—devilish hard. Up goes the curtain, there is a hush all over the theatre, people come on the stage. Then what? It's an eternity—sometimes as much as a quarter of an hour before the audience finds out who's who and what they are all up to.

MANSKY: I never saw such a fellow. Can't you forget the theatre for a single minute?

TURAI: No. That's why I'm such a great dramatist.

MANSKY: You can't be happy for half an hour unless you're talking shop. Life isn't all theatre.

TURAI: Yes, it is—if you write plays. You know what Alphonse Daudet says in his *Memoirs?* When he stood by his father's death-bed, all he could think of was what a wonderful scene it would make for the stage.

MANSKY: It's silly to let your job become an obsession.

TURAI: Well, that's the theatre. Either you master it or it masters you. And of all the brain-racking things in the world, beginning a play is the worst. That's where your technique comes in, my boy. Take this scene here, for instance. We three—Curtain goes up on three ordinary men in dinner jackets. How is anybody to know even that this room we're sitting in is a room in a castle? And how are they to know who we are? If this were a play we would have to start jabbering about a lot of thoroughly uninteresting things until the audience gradually found out who we were.

MANSKY: Well? Why not?

TURAI: Think how much simpler it would be if we were to cut out all that stuff and just introduce ourselves? [*He rises and addresses the audience.*] Ladies and gentlemen, good evening. We three arrived tonight to spend a couple of weeks at this castle. We've just left the dining room where we did ourselves remarkably well with some excellent champagne. My name is Sandor Turai. I am a playwright. I have been a playwright for thirty years. I make a very good thing of it. I bow and step back leaving the stage to you. [*Turai steps back and Mansky steps forward and addresses the audience.*]

MANSKY: Ladies and gentlemen, my name is Mansky—I, too, am a playwright, and this gentleman's lifelong collaborator. We are probably the best known firm in the business.

TURAI: Come to Mansky and Turai for all comedies, farces, and operettas. Satisfaction guaranteed.

MANSKY: I, too, make a very good thing out of it.

TURAI: Which brings us—

MANSKY: —to the remaining member of the trio.

[*They indicate Adam, who rises and addresses the audience in similar fashion but with more diffidence and none of their assurance.*]

ADAM: The last and least. I, ladies and gentlemen, am Albert Adam. I am twenty-five years old and I compose music.

TURAI: Very good music, too.

ADAM: I have done the score for the latest operetta by these two kind gentlemen. My first effort. They discovered me. They got me invited to this castle. Regardless of expense, they bought me a complete wardrobe. Without them I am a complete nonentity. I have no parents, no reputation, and no money.

TURAI: But—you're young.

MANSKY: And gifted.

ADAM: And in love with the prima donna.

TURAI: Don't bother to tell them that. An audience takes if for granted that the young composer is in love with the prima donna. It's tradition.

ADAM: Thank heaven.

TURAI [*again addressing the audience*]: Isn't that the simplest way to begin a play?

MANSKY: Very crude. If that were all there was to it, any fool could write plays.

TURAI: A great many do. But you see how absurdly easy it is—All you have to do is—

MANSKY: All right, all right, all right. For heaven's sake, stop talking shop. I've had enough. Save it for to-morrow.

Avoid scenes in which someone overhears dialogue or sees a piece of business that is of vital importance to him; it cries of coincidence. I know only two ways to make such a situation at all plausible. One is to bring the overhearer into some part of the set that hides him from the others, and to bring him in so far ahead of the crucial line that he stops to listen merely because it is his nature to do so; it then seems a matter of wilful eavesdropping, not coincidence. Another way, which brings suspense, is to plant the eavesdropper somewhere in the set, concealed from the view of the other characters. In *The Lower Depths,* Gorki put Luca asleep on the top of the brick stove before Vassilisa begins to urge Vaska to murder her husband.

Problems of Dialogue

Realism has produced problems in dialogue writing that the earlier playwrights seldom had to face. One of these is to make each of your characters talk in an appropriate idiom. "Each" is perhaps too strong a word, but certainly realistic speech today should reflect as far as possible differences of temperament as well as education. In Shakespeare's tragedies a speech of one chief character is pretty much like that of another. Hamlet and Laertes, Romeo and Juliet, speak in the same fine style. The grave-diggers are something else, of course, and Shakespeare differentiates somewhat between his comedy figures in *Twelfth Night.* Consider, however, the marked differences in character of speech that you find between Morrell, Marchbanks, Lexy, and Burgess, and between Candida and Prossy in Shaw's play. Next to a cliché like "won't you—sit down?" or "I never was more serious in my life," there is nothing so annoying and implausible as the man who talks "out of character"—unless it is such an illusion-shattering remark as Shakespeare let fall from Fabian's lips in *Twelfth Night:* "If this were played upon a stage now, I would condemn it as an improbable fiction."

Obviously you must give the actors dialogue that is easy to speak. You must avoid tongue-twisters and triple alliterations. You should not repeat the same word in a sentence or within two sentences unless the repetition is designed for emphasis. Use simple Anglo-Saxon words unless you want to show that a character is a man of unusual erudition or poise. And let each speech spring from the one before—unless you wish to indicate that a character is self-conscious or distraught.

The dilemma of the realistic playwright is that, as Ervine has said, "The dramatist has to heighten and deepen the common speech, and yet leave it seeming to be common speech . . . has to solve this great problem of keeping his talk agile, lively, life-like, natural, and yet with some artistic appearance to it."

The history of poetic drama in the modern English-speaking theatre is a curious one. Managers and actors of repute in London and New York produced a number of plays by the English poet Stephen Phillips and the American Percy MacKaye during the early part of this century. These writers were stimulated, no doubt, by the Continental vogue of the dramas of Rostand and Maeterlinck, but their plays were not so successful. Perhaps Edward Sheldon was fearful of managerial distrust of the poetic drama when he made his adaptation in 1918 or 1919 of Sem Benelli's *La Cena delle Beffe* under the title of *The Jest.* Although he wrote the dialogue in loose blank verse, he had it typed as if it were normal prose speech. Read almost any line and you will recognize the beat of the iambic rhythm:

Strong, wild, and lustful though their bodies be, my brain will blast them like a bolt from hell. And when last night that vision came to me, came as they bled me like a vile buffoon, it was not agony that made me shriek, but laughter! I laughed! And I laugh still!

The great success of John Barrymore in *The Jest* did not bring forth other efforts in disguised blank verse. In 1930, however, Maxwell Anderson followed his mastery of the realistic play by writing a drama frankly admitting its poetic form—*Elizabeth the Queen.* Its verse, like that in almost all his later plays, was free in rhythm. Some speeches seemed more like prose printed as poetry, but never so prosy as the lines that T. S. Eliot parades as poetic drama in *The Cocktail Party:*

> If there happened to be anyone with you
> I was going to say I'd come back for my
> umbrella. . . .
> I must say you don't seem to be very pleased
> to see me.
> Edward, I understand what has happened
> But I could not understand your manner on
> the telephone.

Another poet, Christopher Fry, has written successful poetic plays for both the London and the New York theatre. His verse in *The Lady's Not for Burning,* for example, is free, yet it is definitely verse:

They also say that I bring back the past;
For instance, Helen comes,
Brushing the maggots from her eyes,
And, clearing her throat of several thousand years,
She says "I loved . . . ;" but cannot any longer
Remember names. Sad Helen. Or Alexander, wearing
His imperial cobwebs and breastplate of shining worms
Wakens and looks for his glasses, to find the empire
Which he knows he put beside his bed.

If, spurred on by the success of Anderson, Eliot, and Fry, the apprentice playwright is tempted to write poetic drama, I suggest that he try loosely rhythmed prose, using the simple words out of the Anglo-Saxon that went into the King James version of the *Bible*. Here are some lines from John Masefield's *Pompey the Great* that show how effective rhythmic prose can be in the theatre of today:

More soldiers. Blow your horns. Spread your colors, ensign. Your colors'll be dust the sooner. Your breath will be in the wind, a little noise in the night. That's what you come to, soldiers. Dust, and a noise in the trees. Dust, and the window rattling. No more flags and horns then . . .

Make the deserts quags of blood, Caesar. Go on in your pride. Till the kings of the world sweep your stables. You'll come to be a dumb thing, tied in a sheet, carried out foot-foremost. You won't know whether it's tar or spice they'll smear you with, to make you burn. And when you're dust, you'll fill a little pot, Caesar, a little metal pot on a shelf. Go pray, man. The primrose the rabbit eats will be a prouder thing than Caesar that day.

10

Testing Your Play Structure

. . . "art consists of hiding art." This old saying is true in its broadest sense . . . the less a spectator realizes the art of a play, the defter must be the play's construction. It must be a labor of pains.

ARTHUR EDWIN KROWS

A MOST IMPORTANT PART OF THE ART OF PLAYWRITING is the concealment of that art. The skeleton of structure must be hidden under the flesh of apparent reality. Because the skeleton is so essential to a play's effectiveness, it is necessary for the student to know how to strip off the deceptive surface, expose the basic structure, and study and appraise it. Certain writers have worked out methods of doing this and of analyzing the organization of the plot to see if it is going to make successful drama. These tests can be applied either to the scenario or to the first draft; you should apply them to both. You can also use them to analyze a produced and printed play in order to see how the writer achieved success.

"The Iron Check List" and "The Golden"

Samuel Selden has named one of these tests the "Iron Check List," and, in order to aid the student in remembering the items he must check, Selden has used words whose first letters spell out "pasto"—the staff of life in Italy. These words are:

PREPARATION [which is largely expositional].
ATTACK [the precipitation of conflict by some word or act].
STRUGGLE [the "guts" of the play, the conflict].
TURN [another name for turning point, major crisis, or climax].
OUTCOME ["the ending . . . how it all works out . . . usually very brief . . . to satisfy the audience that the conflict is really won or lost"].

Selden believes that if a play meets the test of the Iron Check List, it *may* be a successful play, and he believes that most successful plays meet this test. But he recognizes that a play perfectly organized by the Iron Check List may fail if it doesn't meet another test—a test evaluating quality—which he calls the "Golden Check List." Here he has three items:

THEME [which must be unified, acceptable to the audience, and, if unconventional, supported with dialogue and action founded on common premises].
ISSUE [which must be clear, important, interesting].
DRIVE [which is based on the leading character's having a desire that is clear and strong, and that will win sympathy, hold attention, "serve as worthy resistance

to the other man's desire," and join with the desire of the opponent in such a way "as to generate the greatest amount of dramatic heat consistent with the issue of the play"].

If it were not that the opinion of a prejudiced person, the dramatist himself, has to decide whether a play meets the tests of the Iron Check List and the Golden, this might be the true recipe for successful playwriting.

"And, But, and Therefore"

Another test, devised by Miss Gallaway, is based on the fact that "incidents or steps in the course of action can usually be joined by one of three connectives, AND, BUT, and THEREFORE." "And" is usually more common in the first part of a play, and "is likely to indicate sound motivation, plenty of causes." "But" shows contrast, conflict, and suspense. "Therefore" indicates effect, logical coherence, and the consequences or resolution of a situation. Here is how Miss Gallaway analyzes *Elizabeth the Queen:*

Elizabeth and Essex are politically incompatible.	BUT
They love each other uncontrollably.	THEREFORE
They vow never to part.	BUT
Cecil feels that Essex is a threat to England.	THEREFORE
He plots to send Essex away.	AND
Essex's pride causes him to fall into the trap.	THEREFORE

Cecil is able to intercept the correspondence of Elizabeth and Essex. THEREFORE

Essex becomes angry and stages a *coup d' état.* THEREFORE

Elizabeth sends Essex to prison. BUT

Still loving him, she tries to save him. BUT

In prison Essex has realized that he would not make a good king. THEREFORE

He refuses her offer. THEREFORE

Essex must die; Cecil's plot has succeeded.

"Plot and Counterplot"

Krows has devised a test-analysis that he calls "Plot and Counterplot." It applies most effectively to a play in which there are two very clear opposing forces, particularly a hero and a villain, as in *Hamlet:*

HAMLET	KING
Hamlet hears the Ghost's accusation. Makes his vow to avenge his Father's death. Becomes changed.	
	King, feeling guilty, tries to account for change in Hamlet. Polonius suggests it may be just love for his daughter Ophelia, and to satisfy King of this, determines to investigate.

But Hamlet, now having but one purpose in life, breaks with Ophelia.

King, seeing it isn't Ophelia, arranges to sound Hamlet through Hamlet's intimate friends, Rosencrantz and Guildenstern.

In shaking off these two, Hamlet learns that his Uncle suspects him; and, the strolling players arriving, he conceives the idea of using them to test his Uncle.

King, finding Rosencrantz and Guildenstern cannot pump Hamlet, determines with Polonius to learn through Hamlet's Mother.

Hamlet arranges a play paralleling the situation in which he believes his Father was murdered, and "agrees" that the court may witness the performance.

At the performance, the guilty King commits himself.

Hamlet, now satisfied of his Uncle's guilt, determines to kill him; but finding him praying, decides to wait for a more seasonable time.

This gives the King time to plan to rid himself of Hamlet; but he is at loss how to do it because Hamlet is so loved by the people.

Hamlet has the scene with his Mother in which the information sought by the King comes out; but the King's only witness, Polonius, is killed by Hamlet.

This affords the King an excuse for sending Hamlet away; and at the same time he arranges for Rosencrantz and Guildenstern to betray him.

Hamlet agrees to go on account of the death of Polonius; but upon seeing the fine struggle of Fortinbras for the sake of a mere abstract principle, he determines to fight for his own greater purpose, and remains near the King.

The King, finding his plan has failed, tells Laertes to avenge his Father, Polonius, and his Sister, Ophelia (who has gone mad for love of the melancholy prince who has jilted her, and committed suicide), by killing Hamlet.

Hamlet, confronted with his Uncle's perfidy through the attempt of Laertes, is so thoroughly convinced of the guilt of the King that he kills him before his own death from the wound by Laertes.

In modern drama there is seldom as simple an opposition of forces. There is no single hero and no single villain in *Liliom, Journey's End, The Death of a Salesman, Design for Living, The Hasty Heart, Ah, Wilderness!, Candida, The Silver Box, They Knew What They Wanted, Ghosts,* to name only a few. Such plays—like those that do have two characters who may be labeled hero and villain—can be analyzed through listing, scene by scene and act by act, the steps by which the plot moves forward. This is perhaps a combination of Miss Gallaway's "And, But, and Therefore" and Krows' "Plot and Counterplot."

The One-Act Play

Before I give some examples of this sort of analysis, beginning with the one-act play, it may be well to discuss very briefly—or to let others discuss—the difference between the long play and the short. Since the one-acter has to begin late in its story, skillful exposition is of paramount importance. Such a play cannot use more than a situation or two to reach its climax. "A swift development," as Selden says, must lead up to "one well-marked crisis [climax], and then a clean-cut ending . . . there is seldom room for much character change. The chief emphasis throughout, therefore, tends to be on situation and action, all turning on that one point of crisis." "The one-act play," says Finch, "holds no wasted words, it pursues no bypaths, and the playwright uses only what will help to create the effect he desires. Like the short story, its power sometimes lies in implications of life far beyond what is actually shown. It is not a condensed full-length play, and if it is completely written as a one-act play, it cannot be enlarged to a three-act play without losing effectiveness through dilution." It is not nearly so hard to write as the long play, for, as Selden says, "A three-act play is not just three times as hard to write as the one-act; it is nine times as hard."

From 1910 to 1925 there was a very considerable market for good one-act plays in the "little theatres" that sprang up across the country. During the last twenty-five years, this market has shrunk to the smaller amateur groups and the high schools, and the demand has been for plays rather conventional in both form and content. Television is now opening new opportunities to those who wish to write in one act. The content will probably fall between the strict proprieties essential for the high school and the greater freedom of the days of the "little theatre." At present television will use the play written in the normal, one-act form, but, as the new medium develops, it will undoubtedly find that a dramatic technique nearer that of the motion picture will be more effective.

Another Kind of Analysis

In the following pages I have set down a form of analysis that has proved useful to students in understanding the construction of effective "standard" plays and in estimating the values of their own plots. In *The Twelve-Pound Look* it is applied to a play with a trick ending but genuine emotional body. In O'Neill's *In the Zone* and *The Moon of the Caribbees,* this kind of analysis contrasts the "well-made," even theatrical, play with the play of subtle mood and meaning, and brings out the fact that both plays deal with the same material—Smitty's love affair destroyed by drink—but in very different ways. Again, in *A Doll's House* and *Liliom*, the analysis contrasts the complex play with the simple and shows how the two playwrights developed effectively very different patterns of construction.

The Twelve-Pound Look, BY J. M. BARRIE

Sir Harry Sims, self-made and not too well, and his brow-beaten wife, rehearsing for the ceremony of knighthood.	ESTABLISHING CHARACTER AND PROVIDING COMEDY.
Lady Sims and Kate, who, sent by an agency to write replies to congratulatory letters, types a letter that subtly satirizes the attitude of such a social climber as Sir Harry. Lady Sims envies her ability to "do something."	KATE ESTABLISHED AS AN INDEPENDENT PERSON AND LADY SIMS AS LONGING FOR SOMETHING BEYOND HER LIFE.
Kate and Sir Harry. We discover Kate was his first wife, who deserted him leaving a note that	COMPLICATION.
implied she had run away with a lover.	CONFLICT.
Eager to know if it was one of his friends, he agrees to tell her what happened when he found her note if she confesses who the man was.	SUSPENSE.
Sir Harry had been telling some friends that it served an earl right who had not been strong enough to	COMIC EMBARRASSMENT OF SIR HARRY.

keep his wife from running away with a fiddler. Kate confesses that there was no lover. She left because she could not endure his pompous "success."

CONFLICT OF CHARACTER.

To get away, she had rented a typewriter with her savings and when she had earned twelve pounds—the price of the machine—she knew she could support herself, and was free.

PREPARATION FOR THE END OF THE PLAY.

Kate, seeing a portrait of Lady Sims, says she must once have had more character than "the spiritless woman" she had met. She tells him to watch for the "twelve-pound look" coming into his wife's eyes. Kate leaves.

ADDITIONAL PREPARATION.

PREPARATION.

Sir Harry and Lady Sims. He says he has dismissed "that poor lonely wretch." Lady Sims says, "I thought she looked so alive. It was while she was working that machine." Then, inconsequentially: "Are they very expensive?" "What?" "Those machines." She exits, leaving a startled and apprehensive husband.

CLIMAX.

In the Zone, BY EUGENE O'NEILL

In the seamen's forecastle, almost midnight on a day in the year 1915.	
Smitty—an Englishman who seems more a gentleman than a sailor—looks furtively at his shipmates to make sure they are asleep, cautiously opens a suitcase under his bunk, and takes out a black box.	SUSPENSEFUL ACTION.
Another seaman, Davis, about to enter the forecastle, sees Smitty's action, stops to watch.	MINOR COMPLICATION. MORE SUSPENSE.
Scotty, awakening in his bunk, also sees Smitty's action. Smitty hides the black box under the mattress.	ANOTHER SMALL COMPLICATION, WITH ADDED SUSPENSE.
Smitty returns to his bunk, and, snoring, pretends to be asleep.	
Davis, entering, awakens the men.	
We learn that the ship carries ammunition, and that it is entering the war zone where submarines are on the prowl.	EXPOSITION.
One sailor notices that a porthole is open. Scotty and Davis hint at danger from spies.	MINOR COMPLICATION, INCREASING SUSPICION AND SUSPENSE.
As Smitty goes on deck, the men comment on his "Prince of Wales" airs. Davis sets a sailor to watch Smitty and tells how he saw him	EXPOSITION. SUSPENSE.

hide the black box, which Scotty corroborates.	
Jack, another sailor, defends Smitty.	SMALL CONFLICT.
Smitty re-enters, stealthily feels whether his box is safe, and leaves the forecastle.	MORE SUSPICION AND SUSPENSE FOR AUDIENCE.
Some driftwood strikes the hull.	SUSPENSE.
Setting a watch on Smitty, they discuss what to do. They gingerly take the box out of Smitty's bunk and put it in a bucket of water.	SUSPENSE.
Smitty returns. They grab and bind him. When they start to open the box, Smitty struggles and curses until they gag him.	COMPLICATION. PHYSICAL ACTION INTRODUCES A CRISIS.
Instead of a bomb, they find a packet of letters.	COMPLICATION AND A NEW SUSPENSE.
Jack wants to turn Smitty loose.	CONFLICT.
The men discuss how spies use codes to convey information through letters.	NEW SUSPENSE.
They read a letter from a girl who loves Smitty, is going abroad to study singing, and fears he may not have conquered his desire to drink.	COMPLICATION INTRODUCING THE CLIMACTIC SCENE.
Jack objects again.	MINOR CONFLICT ONCE MORE.
A letter addressed to "Sidney Davidson" from Berlin. "Smith" may be "Schmitt."	ANOTHER COMPLICATION.
Another letter, with more love and more worry over liquor. Smitty more and more distraught and pitiful.	THE PATHOS OF SMITTY'S PAST BECOMES CLEAR.

A last letter, written seven months ago, says that the girl has learned of his continued drunkenness, and never wants to see him again. Smitty completely broken. A dried rose falls from the letter. CLIMAX OF SMITTY'S TRAGEDY.

The men untie Smitty, and, in embarrassment, go about their business. RESOLUTION.

The Moon of the Caribbees,

BY EUGENE O'NEILL

The forward deck of a tramp steamer anchored off a West Indies island on a moonlit night. Native music and singing can be heard.

Smitty, an English gentleman turned sailor, is musing sadly. Another seaman kids him about love. INTRODUCTION OF SMITTY'S LOVE STORY.

A woman is to come aboard with several Negro girls; they will have rum hidden in their baskets of fruit. EXPOSITION.

Driscoll, a sailor, announces the price of the rum and warns that there must be no noise or fighting, lest the officers discover the forbidden traffic. PREPARATION FOR THE LATER FIGHT. SUSPENSE ELEMENT.

Smitty says he wishes "they'd stop that song. It makes you think of—well—things you ought to forget." SMITTY'S LOVE STORY AGAIN.

Two sailors start a quarrel, which PREPARATION FOR FIGHT.

goes no further. Driscoll explains that the sailors are to sign for what they buy and the girls will be paid by a ship's officer.	EXPOSITION AND PREPARATION.
The girls arrive. The price for their favors is set.	A CONTRADICTION TO SMITTY'S MOOD.
All but Smitty and another sailor go inside the forecastle so there will be no noise. Pearl, the last girl to go in, tries to date Smitty. He buys a bottle of rum from her and begins to drink.	PREPARATION AGAIN FOR THE FIGHT. PREPARATION FOR THE LATER SCENE BETWEEN PEARL AND SMITTY.
In a dialog between Smitty and an old sailor we learn that Smitty lost a girl of his own class because of drink.	EXPOSITION OF SMITTY'S TRAGIC PAST.
Pearl reappears and makes love to Smitty. He responds momentarily, then turns away and takes another drink.	AN INNER CONFLICT FOR SMITTY.
The men and the girls come out on deck, and a dance begins.	SUSPENSE OVER THE DANGER OF DISCOVERY.
Pearl slaps Smitty.	ANOTHER DEVELOPMENT IN SMITTY'S STORY.
A fight develops between the two seamen who had quarreled. One man is knifed and knocked out. The mate discovers empty rum	THE CLIMAX REACHED IN THE STORY OF THE MEN AND THE GIRLS.

bottles and throws the girls off the boat without pay.

Smitty goes into the forecastle where he can't hear the music from the shore and where there is more liquor.

THE CLIMAX OF SMITTY'S STORY.

A Doll's House, BY HENRIK IBSEN

ACT I. Nora returns to her home with Christmas gifts. Her husband, Torvald, calls her his little squirrel and plays the indulgent father.

ESTABLISHING CHARACTER CONTRASTS IN A HAPPY VICTORIAN HOME.

We learn that he has been made manager of the bank.

PREPARATION FOR HIS RELATIONS WITH MRS. LINDE AND KROGSTAD.

Her little extravagances, which he blames on inheritance.

PREPARATION FOR NORA'S DEBT AND FOR LATER EMPHASIS ON HER EVIL INHERITANCE.

Dr. Rank will come to dinner "as a matter of course."

PREPARATION FOR RANK'S ARRIVAL.

Nora and Mrs. Linde, a widowed friend of former years;

NECESSARY EXPOSITION.

Nora mentions Torvald's illness after their marriage and offers to try to get Torvald to employ Mrs. Linde at the bank.

PREPARATION FOR CRISIS OVER KROGSTAD'S LOSING HIS JOB TO MRS. LINDE.

Nora explains that the seriousness of Torvald's illness had had to be kept from him; so she secretly borrowed the money, something that he would not approve of. She is happy in her secret work to repay the debt.	COMPLICATION AND THREAT OF A CRISIS.
Krogstad, mentioning that he works at the bank, passes on the way to Torvald's study. Mrs. Linde knew him once and is disturbed.	PREPARATION FOR RELATIONS OF MRS. LINDE AND KROGSTAD.
Dr. Rank joins them, mentions his physical illness, and hints at Krogstad's moral disease.	PREPARATION FOR RANK'S DEATH.
Nora asks if Krogstad is in Torvald's power as a bank employee.	PREPARATION FOR KROGSTAD'S BLACKMAIL OF NORA AS WELL AS HER HOPE THAT TORVALD WILL PROTECT HER.
Nora cajoles Torvald into giving Mrs. Linde a job at the bank.	PREPARATION FOR COMPLICATION OF TORVALD'S FIRING KROGSTAD.
Exit all but Nora; enter children, with whom she plays hide-and-seek. Krogstad enters; we learn Nora owes him the money. He says he has seen Mrs. Linde with Torvald; is she to have a job at the bank? Nora boasts it was through	CONTRAST OF NORA'S DOMESTIC HAPPINESS WITH THE SINISTER FIGURE OF KROGSTAD AND THE DANGER OF EXPOSURE.

her influence. Krogstad asks her to use her influence to save his job.	COMPLICATION.
She fears he will tell Torvald about the money she borrowed. Krogstad brings out that she forged the name of her dead father to a security bond. He will expose her if he loses his job. Exit Krogstad.	A STILL MORE IMPORTANT COMPLICATION.
Nora and Torvald, who is upset by Nora's denial of the visit from Krogstad, whom he saw depart.	SLIGHT COMPLICATION IN NORA'S LIFE.
To flatter him Nora asks him to pick her costume for the ball day after tomorrow. Preparing to beg him to spare Krogstad, Nora asks what evil thing the man had done.	PREPARATION FOR TARANTELLA SCENE.
Torvald says it was forgery, makes her promise not to intercede, says that Krogstad is living a deceitful life, and that deceit corrupts children. He exits. Nurse tries to bring in children, but Nora refuses to see them.	FURTHER COMPLICATIONS — KROGSTAD WILL EXPOSE HER OR SHE WILL CORRUPT HER OWN CHILDREN THROUGH DECEIT.
ACT II. Christmas Day. With Nurse, Nora talks of the future of the children without her.	PREPARATION FOR SUICIDE OR LEAVING THE HOME. NORA'S TENSION.
Nora and Mrs. Linde talk of Rank and his disease inherited from a	PREPARATION FOR RANK'S DEATH.
libertine father. An implication that	PREPARATION FOR

Rank and Nora are interested in each other; he is rich.	NORA'S LATER SCENE WITH RANK, IN WHICH SHE TRIES TO ASK FOR MONEY.
Nora again asks Torvald to let Krogstad keep his job. He says he will give it to Mrs. Linde.	DEVELOPMENT OF AN EARLIER COMPLICATION.
Torvald explains the moral superiority of his father to Nora's.	PREPARATION FOR HIS LATER ATTACK ON NORA AS A DECEITFUL, UNWORTHY MOTHER.
He sends a letter of dismissal to Krogstad and tells Nora he has the strength of character to meet any attacks.	APPARENT CLIMAX IS FORESHADOWED. PREPARATION FOR NORA'S BELIEF HE WILL TAKE HER FORGERY ON HIMSELF WHEN IT IS EXPOSED.
Nora and Rank, who says that he must soon die. He will send a card with a black cross when his end is imminent. Nora flirts with Rank, and is about to ask for money when his declaration of love stops this Victorian wife.	PREPARATION. A COMPLICATION THAT PREVENTS A SOLUTION OF HER TROUBLE.
She says that "being with Torvald is a little like being with papa."	PREPARATION FOR HER FINAL RECOGNITION OF HER FALSE

	RELATIONSHIP WITH TORVALD.
Krogstad comments on Torvald's lack of courage.	PREPARATION FOR TORVALD'S LATER FAILURE TO TAKE THE BLAME.
Krogstad speaks of how he once contemplated suicide, and Nora says she fears to kill herself.	PREPARATION.
Krogstad says he has brought a letter telling Torvald the truth and theatening exposure unless he is taken back in a better post.	FURTHER COMPLICATION—AN IMMEDIATE THREAT TO TORVALD.
His statement that he will run the bank through his hold on Torvald moves Nora to face suicide.	PREPARATION FOR NORA'S CONTEMPLATED SUICIDE.
Krogstad, leaving, drops the letter in the locked letter-box.	INTRODUCING A PHYSICAL SYMBOL OF EXPOSURE.
Nora tells Mrs. Linde all, hints at suicide and asks her to tell the truth about the forgery if Torvald takes the blame.	PREPARATION FOR NORA'S BELIEF IN "THE WONDERFUL THING"—THAT TORVALD WILL ASSUME THE FORGERY.
Mrs. Linde says she will appeal to Krogstad, who once would have done anything for her.	SUSPENSE, AND PREPARATION FOR KROGSTAD'S LATER DECISION NOT TO EXPOSE NORA.
Torvald is about to open the letter-	A CRISIS THREATEN-

box, when Nora makes him promise to do nothing for the next twenty-four hours but help her with her dance.	ING EXPOSURE. EXPOSURE AVERTED.
Nora dances, Torvald comments, "as if your life depended upon it."	PHYSICAL ACTION DRAMATIZING HER CRISIS.
Mrs. Linde returns to say that Krogstad is out of town until tomorrow.	A NEW COMPLICATION, CARRYING SUSPENSE.
ACT III. After the costume ball. Mrs. Linde and Krogstad recall their past love and decide to marry.	THE SUBPLOT RESOLVED.
He will ask for his letter back. Mrs. Linde says that Nora and her husband must come to an understanding.	EXPOSURE APPARENTLY AVERTED. A NEW COMPLICATION INSURING EXPOSURE.
Nora, knowing that she will be exposed, determines on suicide. Torvald is amorous. Rank's card announces his approaching death. Nora, still bent on suicide, forces Torvald to read Krogstad's letter. He upbraids her bitterly.	THE APPARENT CLIMAX OF THE PLAY.
A note from Krogstad arrives, saying he will not expose Nora to the world. Torvald reads it and cries, "I am saved," and forgives her as a loving but erring child.	AN IRONIC TWIST THAT DRIVES NORA FROM HIM.

Nora declares she does not love him, that the "wonderful thing" of his assuming her guilt did not happen, that she has been "living here with a strange man." And she leaves him to learn to be an individual.

THE REAL CLIMAX

Liliom, BY FERENC MOLNAR

Where *A Doll's House* is intricate and complex because it is full of complications, *Liliom* is simple in structure, has few complications, yet maintains suspense because of the audience's interest in the relations of the hero and heroine. A subplot of a happy but shallow love furnishes an ironic contrast. A "stunt" play, backed by atmosphere and music, it combines a kind of sublimated realism with philosophical fantasy.

PROLOGUE. A wordless scene at an amusement park with Liliom, as the barker of a merry-go-round, flirting with the girls and threatening their escorts.

SCENE 1. A lonely place in the park where Mrs. Muskat, owner of the merry-go-round, abuses two servant girls, Julie and Marie, for misbehaving with Liliom. Liliom enters, says he will put his arm around any girl he pleases, and Mrs. Muskat fires him.

CHARACTERS ESTABLISHED, THE JEALOUSY OF MRS. MUSKAT, AND THE CALLOUSNESS OF LILIOM.

While he goes to get his things, we learn that Marie is in love with Wolf, who she thinks is a soldier, but who is actually a portier.

THE SUBPLOT BEGINS.

Returning, Liliom asks which one is staying with him. Julie, who will lose her job if she waits longer, decides to stay though Liliom acts indifferent.

COMPLICATION, ESTABLISHING JULIE'S FIXATION ON LILIOM IN SPITE OF HIS BEHAVOIR AND REPUTATION.

Two policemen tell her that Liliom picks up servant girls, takes their money, and deserts them. Julie sticks by Liliom, who hints at marriage and reformation.

SUSPENSE AS TO FUTURE HAPPINESS.

SCENE 2. A cheap photographic studio where Liliom and Julie live with her aunt. Liliom has been arrested twice in two months for fighting.

EXPOSITION.

Marie talks amusingly of her love for Wolf.

SUBPLOT CONTRAST.

Liliom has slapped Julie when she asked him why he wouldn't go back to work for Mrs. Muskat.

EXPOSITION OF CHARACTER CLASH.

A widowed carpenter wants to marry Julie.

SUSPENSE.

Mrs. Muskat comes to urge Liliom to return to the park. He, who has entered with a thief, Ficsur, is on the point of agreeing when Julie,

PREPARATION FOR THE ROBBERY. SUSPENSE.

getting him alone, tells him they are to have a baby.	COMPLICATION.
Liliom drives Mrs. Muskat away, and asks Ficsur about the robbery he had planned.	MORE PREPARATION FOR THE ROBBERY. SUSPENSE.
SCENE 3. The same. Ficsur plans the robbery with Liliom, while Julie goes about her household duties and a policeman gets his photograph taken.	CONTINUED PREPARATION AND SUSPENSE. A SUGGESTION OF THE LAW'S MENACE.
Liliom, worried about the crime, talks of judgment in heaven, and Ficsur says he will appear before a police magistrate, not God.	PREPARATION FOR SCENE IN HEAVEN.
Liliom takes a carving knife. Julie feels it under his coat and asks him to stay home. He leaves. She denies to her aunt that Liliom took her knife.	SUSPENSE OVER THE ROBBERY.
Marie and Wolf have their photos taken.	SUBPLOT AGAIN.
SCENE 4. A railroad embankment. Liliom talks of the romance that the railroad train and the telegraph wires hold for him.	A SYMPATHETIC CHARACTER-NOTE.
Ficsur and Liliom play cards and Liliom loses all the money he may make from the robbery.	IRONIC FORESHADOWING OF TRAGEDY.
The cashier appears. The robbery	SUSPENSE.

miscarries. Liliom, about to be arrested, "bursts into laughter, half defiant, half self-pitying," cries, "Julie!" and stabs himself. We do not know if he is dead.

COMPLICATION.

SCENE 5. The studio again. Liliom, dying, tells Julie he slapped her because he couldn't bear to see her crying on his account.

CONFLICT OF CHARACTER RESTATED.

Julie talks with Marie and Wolf, agreeing that Liliom wasn't a good man and that she will forget him in a year. Mrs. Muskat enters and tries to give Julie money she owes Liliom. She says she loved Liliom better than Julie did, and Julie agrees.

SUBPLOT.

Alone with Liliom's body, Julie tells him that she loves him: "You bad, bad boy—I love you—I never told you before—I was ashamed."

JULIE'S DEEP LOVE EXPOSED.

The carpenter enters to renew his plea, but Julie refuses.

JULIE'S LOVE DEMONSTRATED.

Two angels come for Liliom: "Until you are quite forgotten, you will not be finished with the earth."

PREPARATION FOR SCENE IN HEAVEN.

SCENE 6. A magistrate's court in heaven, where dead men are told that they have a chance to return

PREPARATION FOR

to earth to do a good deed and gain forgiveness in heaven. Through the magistrate's questioning of Liliom we realize his great love for Julie and the stubborn pride that made him beat her when he knew she was right. He will not say he is sorry.

LILIOM'S ATTEMPT TO DO A GOOD DEED. ANOTHER EXPLANATION OF LILIOM'S CHARACTER AND HIS CONFLICT WITH JULIE.

The magistrate tells him he will burn for sixteen years and then have a chance to return to earth and do a good deed. Liliom is still defiant.

PREPARATION FOR FINAL SCENE.

SCENE 7. Julie's home sixteen years later. Marie and Wolf, who now run a restaurant. Liliom enters, and is told by his child that her father went to America to work, and died there. Liliom says he knew her father and that he beat Julie. Julie denies this. "He was always good to me." Julie tells the child to send him away. He tries desperately to do a trick for her or give her a star he has stolen from heaven. The child points for him to go and he slaps her hand. Julie asks who he is. He says he is a poor, tired beggar who took her soup and slapped her child. "Are you angry with me?"

SUBPLOT FOR CONTRAST.

SUSPENSE OVER LILIOM'S FATE.

COMPLICATION LEADING TO RESOLUTION OF THE PLAY AND THE THEME.

"Jesus protect me—I don't understand it—I'm not angry—not angry at all—" After Liliom has gone, Julie says she had somehow thought of the child's father. The child asks, "Has anyone ever hit you without hurting you in the least?" Julie: "Someone may beat you and beat you and beat you—and not hurt you at all."

A FINAL SCENE OF RESOLUTION IN WHICH WE REALIZE FULLY THE GREAT LOVE OF JULIE AND LILIOM.

A Cautionary Epilogue

I wish the stage were as narrow as the wire of a tight-rope dancer, so that no incompetent would dare step upon it.

GOETHE

IF ALL THESE WORDS HAVE NOT CONVINCED YOU THAT playwriting is far too difficult and dangerous an occupation, an occupation fraught with labor and heartbreak, consider what you face when your play is accepted for production, and passes into the hands of producer, director, scene designer, actors, critics, and audiences.

In pointing out the difference between writing and playwriting, Jesse Lynch Williams once said:

. . . There must be some reason for the theatre! For when an author can convey his ideas through the two processes of reading and writing, it seems a wicked waste of time, thought, and money to employ actors, directors, scene-painters, costumers, electricians, musicians, carpenters, ushers, and ticket-sellers. Telling a story, like painting a picture, is a one-man job. But the playwright, like the architect, arrives at his ultimate objective only through the work of other crafts, expert and otherwise. What gets through the three-ply screen of manager, director, and actor, may be better, but it is not so much his own. He is both helped and handicapped by human and material mediums which the novelist can blithely ignore. . . . [A successful playwright once said,] "Why anyone who can write anything else, including advertisements, insurance, or bad checks, deliberately prefers the indignities of the drama is beyond me." He swears he will never write another. His friends do not believe him.

Samson Raphaelson writes:

The only justification for a man in his right mind being a playwright is that it's the one thing he does best and gets the most satisfaction from doing. There is every other reason in the world why every playwright I know should not go near the theatre again. You are taking the most ungodly risks.

Appendices

Type Style for Play Manuscripts

THERE ARE TWO CHIEF STYLES IN WHICH PLAYS APpear. In printed anthologies, where economy of space is essential, the name of the character is printed on the same line as his speech, and various other efforts are made to save paper by condensation. The typists who prepare manuscripts for submission to agents or managers use a style that is much more open.

The following pages use the latter style of typing. I should advise the beginner to adopt it even for his first drafts. One of its advantages is that, unless there are an unusual number of stage directions on a page, the page is about one minute long in playing time. This gives you a rough idea of the length of your scenes and acts, as well as the whole play.

Incidental business or indications of emotion having to do with the character who speaks a line are indented 8 or 10 spaces and enclosed in parentheses. Longer descriptions of business or setting or stage directions having to do with other characters are indented to the center line and do not have to be so enclosed.

The two pages of dialogue in the sample are from different acts.

If you wish to describe the people of the play at more length on the page marked "Cast of Characters," do so, but be sure to repeat each description or amplify it in the scene in which the character first appears.

Be sure to be as explicit as possible in listing the setting and time of day of each scene in the "Synopsis of Scenes," repeating this information in the script itself.

If the cast of characters is short, the synopsis of scenes may be placed below it on a single page.

On each page type the number of the act and the scene, if there is more than one scene to an act. Then add the page number of the scene and the page number for the whole script. For example: II–14–35 for the 14th page of the second act and the 35th page of the whole script, or, if there is more than one scene in an act, II–2–14–85 for the 14th page of the second scene of act two and the 85th page of the whole script. Use Roman numerals only for the acts.

The play used, *Murder in a Nunnery,* is actually a dramatization by Emmet Lavery of a novel by Eric Shepherd. The credit to Mr. Shepherd has been eliminated in order to show the customary title page for an original play. I am indebted to Mr. Lavery and his publisher, Samuel French, for permission to reprint these pages.

MURDER IN A NUNNERY

by

EMMET LAVERY

May, 1945
(or--
Revised
August, 1945.)

CAST OF CHARACTERS

CELEBRANT AT VESPERS

ALTAR BOY

THE BARONESS

MRS MOSS

MOTHER PEAGLE

MOTHER PECK

SERGEANT PAT MULLIGAN

REVEREND MOTHER

INSPECTOR ANDREW J PEARSON

ANGELA

VERITY

INEZ

TURKEY

PRUDENCE

MOTHER TREVOR

MOTHER BASSONWAITE

REPORTER

MR TURTLE

NUNS

* * *
* *
*

SYNOPSIS OF SCENES

ACT ONE

(First Day)

Scene 1: Chapel

Scene 2: Reverend Mother's Parlor

Scene 3: Bedroom of Baroness

ACT TWO

(Second Day)

Scene 1: Reverend Mother's garden - morning

Scene 2: Reverend Mother's garden - afternoon

Scene 3: Reverend Mother's garden - evening

ACT THREE

(Third Day)

Scene 1: Reverend Mother's Parlor

Scene 2: The same, a few moments later (or about 10 minutes later)

THE TIME is the present

I - 3 - 1 - 20

ACT ONE

Scene Three

The Baroness' bedroom; several hours later, the same evening.

The room has a certain charm and distinction The dominant piece of furniture is a rather royal bed up center, topped by lemon and green draperies and a coat-of-arms, flanked by torcheres at head of the bed. In a unit setting the bed masks the center arch. The side arches take drapes and full length terrace windows open out on a terrace. At the foot of bed is a small trunk rest. On the walls are some good prints. Double doors give entrance to the room down right and left. The main lighting in the room is controlled by switch at doors down right which also regulates lights in the torcheres at bed. A small lamp on the Baroness' desk up left is controlled by a button on the lamp standard. Doors down right lead to a main hall of the school. Doors at left lead to other rooms in the suite of Baroness, including the bedroom of MRS. MOSS.

AS THE CURTAIN GOES UP, we see that the drapes in the room are drawn. Torcheres are lit; so also the little lamp on the desk of Baroness. There the SERGEANT, sitting in a cramped position, is making painful little notes in a dog-eared book. INSPECTOR is smoking thoughtfully as he moves about room.

Inspector

And the knife that was used -- where did that come from?

Sergeant

Just an ordinary gardener's tool, sir.

Inspector

And the gardener?

Reverend Mother (cont.) II - 1 - 10 - 40

of importance has been found?

Mother Trevor

(Eagerly)
No - not quite, Mother. But the Inspector is going to search the cemetery for something - I'm not sure just what - I don't think he is either - but he said I might go along with him. Is that permissible, Mother?

Reverend Mother

(Smoothly)
Of course - of course -
(Moving up to them)
- but I think I should like to go along too, if you have no objections, Inspector?

Inspector

(A little puzzled)
Not at all - charmed, I'm sure. Charmed!

INSPECTOR moves out up back with the two NUNS. The head of INEZ appears in the gateway down left. She tip-toes over quickly to center, then moves up and down as if still doing a penance - but keeping an eye on the figures moving out up back.

Inez

Meditation bathes the soul - 256. Meditation bathes the soul - 257. Meditation bathes the soul - 293.

Down right the face of JOHNNY GUEST, a London reporter appears atop the garden wall. He is a transplanted American tabloid lad - about 35, with a dry and tempered air about him. In his hand is a small camera.

All right - hold it a second - just looking off into the East a bit - fine -!

Instinctively INEZ finds herself obeying the command.

Inez

Who are you? What do you want here anyway?

BIBLIOGRAPHICAL REFERENCES

Anderson, Maxwell. *The Essence of Tragedy and Other Footnotes and Papers.* Washington, D. C.: Anderson House, 1939.

Archer, William. *Play-making: A Manual of Craftsmanship.* New York: Dodd, Mead and Co., Inc., 1937.

Aristotle. "Poetics," Theodore Buckley, tr., in *European Theories of the Drama.* New York: Crown Publishers, 1947.

Art of Playwriting, The: Lectures Delivered at the University of Pennsylvania on the Mask and Wig Foundation. Philadelphia: University of Pennsylvania Press, 1928.

Baker, George Pierce. *Dramatic Technique.* Boston & New York: Houghton Mifflin Co., 1919.

Brunetière, Ferdinand. "The Law of the Drama," Philip Hayden, tr., in *European Theories of the Drama.* New York: Crown Publishers, 1947.

Castelvetro, Lodovico. "Miscellaneous Critical Works," in *European Theories of the Drama.* New York: Crown Publishers, 1947.

Clark, Barrett H., ed. *European Theories of the Drama.* New York: Crown Publishers, 1947.

Corneille, Pierre. "First Discourse on the Uses and Elements of Dramatic Poetry," Beatrice Stewart MacClintock, tr., in *European Theories of the Drama.* New York: Crown Publishers, 1947.

Darlington, W. A. *The Actor and His Audience.* London & Toronto: Phoenix House, Ltd., 1949.

Dunsany, Edward John, 18th Baron. "The Carving of the Ivory," in *The Art of Playwriting.* Philadelphia: University of Pennsylvania Press, 1928.

Egri, Lajos. *The Art of Dramatic Writing.* New York: Simon & Schuster, 1946.

Eliot, T. S. "Poetry and Drama," in *The Atlantic,* 187:30–37. Boston: The Atlantic Monthly Co., 1951.

Elwood, Maren. *Write the Short Story.* Boston: The Writer, Inc., 1947.

Ervine, St. John. *How to Write a Play.* New York: Macmillan Co., 1928.

European Theories of the Drama. Barrett H. Clark, ed. New York: Crown Publishers, 1947.

Finch, Robert. *How to Write a Play.* New York: Greenberg, 1948.

Freytag, Gustav. "The Technique of the Drama," Elias J. MacEwan, tr., in *European Theories of the Drama.* New York: Crown Publishers, 1947.

Gallaway, Marian. *Constructing a Play.* New York: Prentice-Hall, Inc., 1950.

Galsworthy, John. "Some Platitudes Concerning Drama," in *The Inn of Tranquillity: Studies and Essays.* New York: Charles Scribner's Sons, 1912.

Goldoni, Carlo. See van Steenderen.

Hopkins, Arthur. *How's Your Second Act?* New York: Samuel French, 1948.

Ibsen, Henrik. *From Ibsen's Workshop.* (*Collected*

Works of Henrik Ibsen, William Archer, ed., Vol. XII.) A. G. Chater, tr. New York: Charles Scribner's Sons, 1924.

Jouvet, Louis. "Success: The Theatre's Only Problem," in *Theatre Arts Anthology*. New York: Theatre Arts Books: Robert M. MacGregor, 1950.

Krows, Arthur Edwin. *Playwriting for Profit.* New York: Grosset & Dunlap, 1928.

Lawson, John Howard. *Theory and Technique of Playwriting and Screen Writing*. New York: G. P. Putnam's Sons, 1949.

Lessing, Gotthold Ephraim. "Hamburg Dramaturgy," E. C. Beasley & Helen Zimmern, trs., in *European Theories of the Drama*. New York: Crown Publishers, 1947.

Lindsay, Howard. "Notes on Playwriting," in *Theatre Arts Anthology*. New York: Theatre Arts Books: Robert MacGregor, 1950.

Lope de Vega. *The New Art of Writing Plays in This Age,* William T. Brewster, tr. New York: Dramatic Museum of Columbia University, 1914.

Mitchell, Langdon. "Substance and Art in the Drama," in *The Art of Playwriting*. Philadelphia: University of Pennsylvania Press, 1928.

Price, William Thompson. *Analysis of Play Construction and Dramatic Principle*. New York: W. T. Price, Publisher, 1908.

Raphaelson, Samson. *The Human Nature of Playwriting*. New York: Macmillan Co., 1949.

Rowe, Kenneth Thorpe. *Write That Play*. New York: Funk & Wagnalls, 1939.

Schlegel, Wilhelm August. "Lectures on Dramatic Art and Literature," John Black, tr., in *European Theories of the Drama*. New York: Crown Publishers, 1947.

Selden, Samuel. *An Introduction to Playwriting*. New York: F. S. Crofts & Co., 1946.

Strindberg, August. Preface to "Miss Julia," in *Plays by August Strindberg, Second Series,* Edwin Björkman, tr. New York: Charles Scribner's Sons, 1920.

Thompson, Alan Reynolds. *The Anatomy of Drama*. Berkeley & Los Angeles: University of California Press, 1946.

van Steenderen, F. C. L. *Goldoni on Playwriting*. New York: Dramatic Museum of Columbia University, 1919.

Williams, Jesse Lynch. "Writing and Playwriting," in *The Art of Playwriting*. Philadelphia: University of Pennsylvania Press, 1928.

Index